FONDUES
from
Around the World

Nearly 200 Recipes for Fish, Cheese and Meat Fondues •
Oriental Hot Pots • Tempura • Sukiyaki • Dessert Fondues

Eva and Ulrich Klever

New York • London • Toronto • Sydney

Credits

Helen Feingold, translation and Americanization
Maureen Reynolds, recipe testing
Patricia Connell, editing

Teuber-Studio, color photographs
Peter Schimmel, drawings

About the authors

Eva and Ulrich Klever have worked together as food writers for
many years. Well known in Germany for his weekly cooking
column in *Spiegel* and then in *Frau Im Spiegel,* Ulrich has been
supplying German cooks with his favorite recipes for over 14 years,
while his wife has managed the test kitchen in which all the recipes
are prepared. Together they have written two other books on food,
one about baking bread and another extolling the virtues of
homemade specialties. Over the years they have collected and
written many fondue recipes, as they travel around the world in
search of its infinite variations. They have assembled here a
collection of fondue recipes that will surprise you with its versatility
and variations, from the traditional Swiss cheese fondue to hearty
French fare, and from oriental hotpots to sukiyaki and tempura.

First English-language edition published 1984 by
Barron's Educational Series, Inc.

©1980 by Gräfe and Unzer GmbH, Munich, West Germany

The title of the German edition is
Das Grosse Buch der Fondues.

All inquiries should be addressed to:
Barron's Educational Series, Inc.
250 Wireless Boulevard
Hauppauge, New York 11788

International Standard Book No. 0-8120-5454-7

Library of Congress Cataloging in Publication Data
Klever, Eva.
    Fondues from Around the World.
    Translation of: Das Grosse Buch Der Fondues.
    Includes index.
    1. Fondue I. Klever, Ulrich, 1922- 4X. II. Title.
TX825.K5513 1984   641.8   84-9159
ISBN 0-8120-5454-7

Printed in Hong Kong
78   490   9876

Contents

THE CENTER OF SOCIABILITY

About 15 years ago cheese fondue crossed the borders of Switzerland to spread fondue fever through the rest of the Western world. Then came the oil fondues in which meat and, later, fish were cooked. Westerners began to take a new look at the ancient Chinese firepot, which uses broth to cook shellfish, chicken, and vegetables, and at-table cooking became the favorite of people with all sorts of different tastes and habits. That's because fondue is fun.

Today, cooking at the table around the fondue pot or Chinese firepot is a perfect setting for both family and guests. A fondue party requires little previous preparation, since guests do the cooking themselves. The table is set; the cheese mixture cooks gently, the broth simmers, or the oil gets hot. The accompaniments are ready, and the diners—including the host—sit around the table. For two hours, everyone is occupied with eating, dipping, talking, and drinking.

This book is about fondues. The first chapter gives you the fondue fundamentals. We have tried to anticipate all possible errors and guide you in ways to avoid them, so your fondues will be as successful as possible. Further on in the book we list and describe varieties to suit every taste. We offer advice on accompanying wines, and we also have special bread recipes should you wish to make the bread for dipping. We survey some fondue sauce recipes and describe various fondue pots and other equipment on the market.

We hope that this book can answer all the questions you have as you prepare a fondue or enjoy any other type of at-table cooking. We wish you lots of fun and satisfaction!

NOTE: All recipes are for 4 servings, except where otherwise noted.

FONDUE— WHAT IS IT?

In French, the verb *fondre* means "to melt." Therefore, the word *fondue*, "melted," is accurate when describing a cheese fondue and all its variations. But the word is also often used to describe other classic dishes, including chicken fondue (poached chicken in cream sauce), tomato fondue (tomato sauce), as well as cheese fillings for tortes, croquettes, and pancakes. The cheese fondue as we know it comes from Switzerland—understandably, since this country produces such good melting cheese. Legend has it that fondue came about during the Reformation, when the Protestant canton of Zurich was battling the surrounding Catholic cantons. Provisions were scarce, and people were hungry. One side put forth a large tub of milk; the other side contributed cheese, which was crumbled into the milk, and also brought some crusts of bread; thus, it is said, fondue was born.

After World War II, Swiss gourmets cooked pieces of meat by dunking them in hot oil, and they ate as they would a cheese fondue. They called it *fondue bourguignonne*, since the French-speaking Swiss are descendants of the Burgundians. Since then the word *fondue* has been applied to all foods that are cooked in a pot at the table, then dipped into various sauces. Purists occasionally want to return to the correct sense of the word, but in this book we take its widest meaning: fondues themselves, plus tempura, hot pots, sukiyaki and other recipes.

Entertaining with Fondue

With a fondue as the centerpiece of your party, you can achieve maximum results with minimum effort. Fondue sets a good mood; a humorist once wrote, "In a country where people eat fondue, there can be no wars." When we are eating from a single pot—by dunking in our pieces of bread or meat or vegetables—we cannot argue. We concentrate on the meal at hand, relaxing and chatting between bites. The dinner lasts longer, and everyone is relaxed and friendly. Fondue is perfect party food!

The fondue party is probably a latter-day version of the primitive huddling around a fire, with blazing logs in a clearing on the shore transformed to the blue flame of a tabletop burner. Whether your guests dip their crusts of bread in cheese or fry chunks of meat in hot oil or boiling broth, fondue is different and special. The simple meal becomes routine, the newcomer is welcomed, and everyone is bound by the magic of the fire. Your guests will dip into the past and forget the pressures of the day. As a host or hostess, your graciousness will be remembered and appreciated.

Some Fondue Tips

For a proper fondue, there must be at least two persons, since eating out of the pot alone would contradict the basic nature of this sociable meal. Do not seat more than six persons around the pot. With more than six, there is no room for all the forks; also, the fondue cheese or oil cools too much and is eaten too quickly.

Make your table colorful. The covering should be rustic and bright. But whether you use place settings on a bare table or a tablecloth, have accessories that harmonize or contrast with the serving dishes. If possible, capture the natural outdoor essence of fondue in dishes decorated with wildflowers. You can use almost any kind of accessories, of course, but silver and crystal seem a bit out of place with a fondue pot.

Have napkins and even bibs for your guests, since sometimes a fondue can splatter or drip from the fork. For every fondue, a pepper mill also belongs on the table.

Have the bread in pretty baskets lined with napkins or bright cloths. If you have dipping sauces as part of your meal, serve them in small saucers or bowls.

Equipment

Numerous pots and pans, which can be placed on all kinds of burners, are available for making fondue. Pots are made for every taste—there are many choices for fans of cast-iron; there are easy-care pots for practical people; and lovers of the rustic and colorful can purchase all sorts of attractive pots. The prices range from inexpensive to very expensive: judge for yourself among the pots available in gourmet housewares shops.

For a cheese fondue only an earthenware pot is required, as the temperatures involved are moderate. Be certain the pot is of good quality and is not cracked, or else you are likely to spill melted cheese onto the burner or tablecloth.

Meat fondues, which are cooked at a higher temperature than cheese, require metal pots. Enameled cast-iron pots are ideal; they are excellent for cheese fondues as well.

In addition to the pot, you need long-tined forks—one fork per person for a cheese fondue and two per person for a meat fondue (one fork goes into the hot oil and the other removes the food from the hot fork to prevent burning the lips). The original cheese fondue fork had three tines, while the meat fork had two with small barbs. Nowadays, you'll see many variations on both.

Do not use all-metal skewers, even though they may be attractive, since the metal heats up and can burn your fingers as you hold it. Wooden skewers are preferred and actually required with certain types of fondue. For more information on fondue equipment, see pages 132-134.

Heat Sources

The candle is the smallest heat and is perfect for a chocolate fondue. Most burners, however, are fueled with alcohol. An alcohol burner is the hottest tabletop heat source, the height of the flame determined by controlling the amount of air let into the container. With a high flame, one filling of alcohol will last 60 to 80 minutes; with a small flame, about 2½ hours. Alcohol burns without smoke, a great advantage. Be careful, however, to choose a burner that will operate without problems. It should light easily and should not turn on its stand.

There are also gas burners, which use butane and are quite efficient. One filling will burn for an hour at a high flame; at medium, it will burn for three hours, and on low, for nine hours. Butane also burns without smoke, and the burner can be regulated very accurately. For safety reasons, butane heaters are sold only with special stands.

The newer electric fondue sets are very practical. All types of fondues can be prepared in them, including chocolate mixtures. The burners need only be turned to the correct setting and the heat is regulated automatically. For a cheese fondue, the setting should be from 1 to 4 (170°F or 85°C). For an oil fondue, select number 6 (350°F or 180°C). For broth, use number 6 until it comes to a boil, then simmer at number 4 or 5 (200°F or 100°C). For a chocolate fondue, use setting number 2 or 3 (150°F or 70°C). The only drawback of this type of heater is that it lacks a romantic flame.

Accompanying Beverages

It is likely you will serve wine with your fondue; if so, then choose the same wine as was used to prepare the fondue. Some people, however, prefer not to drink chilled wine with hot cheese. You will find it best to have your wine, especially if red, at room temperature or only slightly cooler. See page 131 for more information on wine choices.

Other beverages appropriate with fondue range from hot black tea (especially for the Oriental fondues) to kirsch or another brandy (particularly when there is brandy in the fondue). Often the bread cubes are dunked into the fondue, then dipped in the kirsch; this method is called "sans-souci." A sip from the glass when the fondue is half eaten is called "the drink in the middle."

Some Fondue Rituals

European fanciers believe that whoever serves his guests a glass of wine and a few slices of prosciutto with pepper knows what is proper and tastes good. Prosciutto can be nibbled during a fondue party.

When the cheese fondue is almost finished, a brown crust will form on the bottom of the pot. Do not let it burn; remove the pot from the heat, loosen the crust with a fork and give it to the honored guest or divide it among the group.

When the flame dies, have your guests remain seated for a short while, drinking one or more glasses of brandy and nibbling on leftover pieces of bread. After a short pause, serve coffee or a chilled sweet wine.

Helpful Hints

- For a cheese fondue, use caution in adding cheese rinds. They should only constitute one-third of the cheese mixture or the flavor will be too sharp.
- Add fresh herbs at the table; dried herbs should be pulverized and pre-mixed with the fondue. Add the herbs gradually. For rich color in cheese fondue, stir in just enough soaked saffron threads or turmeric to give a delicate flavor.
- An oil fondue is best served in an airy place such as a balcony or terrace.
- If you are a beginner at fondues, try one out with your family first. It is harder to experiment with guests.
- Season the meat and fish pieces for an oil fondue after cooking. When hot, the meat quickly absorbs flavor. Avoid salting meat during dunking in oil, since it can make the hot oil splatter. Add pepper and dried or fresh herbs after cooking also; if added earlier the herbs will fall off into the hot oil and burn.
- For a broth fondue, cook the dried herbs in the liquid but add fresh herbs at the table. Or sprinkle the pieces of meat with the herbs if you do not wish the broth to get stronger in flavor.
- Prepare attractive garnishes for your fondue table. Thin slices of mushroom, gherkin, or, if you're feeling extravagant, truffle, can be cut into decorative shapes and floated in the fondue pot.

MELT DOWN!

The Basic Cheese Fondue and Variations

It all began with cheese. In this chapter we give you the basic recipe, then offer multiple variations including the popular raclette. Read the basic recipe to learn all about it, including the best type of pot to use, how to combine your ingredients, and what to do if something goes wrong.

Basic Recipe

Neuchâtel Fondue

Picture, page 18

Ingredients:

½ clove garlic

1 pound (450 g) Gruyère cheese

8 ounces (225 g) Emmentaler cheese

1½ cups (⅜ l) dry white wine (Neuchâtel is best)

1 teaspoon fresh lemon juice

4 teaspoons cornstarch

1½ tablespoons (2 cl) kirsch

2 to 3 turns of a pepper mill

pinch of freshly grated nutmeg

How to prepare:

Before its first use, an unglazed clay fondue pot should have a mixture of milk and water cooked in it to season it. Glazed ceramic or enameled cast iron can be used without seasoning. Rub the inside of the pot with cut surface of garlic. Coarsely grate the cheese and mix them in the pot. Add wine, lemon juice, and cornstarch and stir over medium heat until cheese melts (this should be done on the kitchen range). The lemon juice is important, as it gives a flavorful tang and encourages the cheese to melt quickly. Stir with a wooden spoon in a figure 8 motion to keep the cheese from getting stringy.

Stir in kirsch, pepper and nutmeg, and cook a bit longer until mixture is smooth and creamy. Transfer the pot to the burner on the table, where the fondue can simmer.

To serve:

Spear bite-size cubes of bread on a fork and dunk into the cheese. Stir until bread is well coated, then remove while rotating fork to keep cheese from dripping. Careful—the cheese is hot!

The cheese fondue should continue to cook lightly during the entire meal. An experienced fondue eater stirs the cheese each time he dips a piece of bread; in this way the fondue will stay creamy right down to the bottom.

Important:

Measure cornstarch carefully. Four level teaspoons weigh ⅓ ounce (10 g), but if heaped high can weigh almost ½ ounce (12 g).

Bread for a Cheese Fondue

Allow 4 slices or 7 ounces (200 g) for each person. We use a crusty Italian or French bread and cut it into bite-size cubes; make sure each cube has some crust, so the bread is held firmly on the fork and does not fall off in the fondue. For a man, the penalty for dropping the bread into the fondue is paying for more wine or for the next fondue; a woman can pay with a kiss.

The bread should not be too fresh, but neither should the cubes be all dried out. For this reason, it is best cut shortly before serving; for longer storage, wrap in foil.

When Something Goes Wrong

If the fondue is too thick: While it is cooking beat in a little warmed wine or kirsch.

If the fondue is too thin: Stir in a handful of grated cheese over medium heat. Or thicken with a little cornstarch which has been mixed with white wine.

If there are lumps: Try adding a bit more lemon juice or white wine vinegar; stir well to blend.

If the cheese and wine separate: Replace on range and cook at high heat while beating with a whisk. At the table, make sure the cheese is stirred each time bread is dunked. The fondue will only separate if you and your guests forget to stir frequently. Stir with the bread, scraping the bottom to make sure the fondue does not burn.

If the cheese and wine mixture is not smooth: Dissolve 1 teaspoon cornstarch in a little wine and lemon juice. Whisk into fondue.

If you have not prepared enough fondue: When the fondue is half finished, stir in 2 or 3 well-beaten eggs, season heavily with pepper and, if desired, garlic salt, and reduce the burner flame. This will increase the volume of the mixture for further dipping.

If fondue is left over: Cover with cold water and let fondue harden, then remove from the pot.

Which Wine and Which Cheese?

In this recipe collection you will learn about the various wines with which you can prepare different cheese fondues. Use German wines with a yellow label reading *Trocken*, or Dry. In general, a wine that is high in acid makes a better cheese fondue than a sweet wine. Lemon juice (or wine vinegar) is added to compensate for wines that have too low an acid content. Certain Swiss wines are perfect—Neuchâtel, wines from Fendant, the lake districts of Biel and Murten, from the Zurich region, and from Lake Geneva (Lac Léman). A good apple wine or dry cider is also suitable. See page 131 for more information on which wines are best to drink with fondue.

Keep in mind that the less aged a cheese is, the milder the flavor it will give a fondue; more aging produces a heartier taste. See page 35 "Principal Fondue Cheeses," for suggestions.

Once you have mastered the basic recipe, it will not be difficult to prepare those that follow. We will begin with special fondues from the various Swiss cantons and cities.

12

Favorite Cheese Fondues

Freiberger Fondue

An alcohol-free fondue without wine or kirsch.

Ingredients:

1¾ pounds (800 g) aged Vacherin à Fondue

1 clove garlic, halved

butter

¼ cup (6 cl) warm water

cornstarch (optional)

freshly ground pepper

salt

How to prepare:

Freiberger Vacherin is a mild, easily melted cheese which can be found during the winter months in specialty stores and delicatessens (see page 35). If you can't locate it, substitute French Vacherin. Cut the cheese into small pieces or thin slices, rub the inside of the fondue pot with the clove of garlic and brush with butter. Add the cheese and warm water, place over low heat and mash and stir the cheese constantly with a fork; do not allow the mixture to bubble. If the fondue becomes too hot, mix a little cornstarch with water and stir a small amount at a time into the fondue until smooth. If the mixture is too thick, add a few spoonfuls of warm water. Season with pepper and salt. Transfer pot to a candle warmer or tabletop burner set on low heat.

To serve:

Try dipping the pieces of bread into plum brandy before dunking in cheese.

Pussyfoot Fondue

This alcohol-free American fondue was named after prohibitionist "Pussyfoot" Johnson.

Ingredients:

9 ounces (250 g) Gruyère cheese

9 ounces (250 g) Emmentaler cheese

1 clove garlic, halved

1 cup (¼ l) apple juice

1 tablespoon cornstarch

3 tablespoons (4 cl) fresh lemon juice

sweet paprika

freshly grated nutmeg

How to prepare:

Grate the cheeses. Rub the fondue pot with garlic. Add the apple juice and heat slowly. When it just begins to bubble, stir in the cheese by the handful. When cheese is melted, mix cornstarch and lemon juice until smooth. Stir into cheese mixture until thickened. Season with paprika and nutmeg. Transfer to tabletop burner.

To serve:

This is best served with cubes of French bread (see recipe, page 129).

Fondue Vaudoise

One of many cheese fondue variations from around Zurich, this is of a thinner consistency than most.

Ingredients:

1 pound 5 ounces (600 g) Gruyère cheese (use several, of various degrees of aging)

1 clove garlic

butter

1½ cups (⅜ l) Vaudois wine (La Côte or Dorin)

1 teaspoon fresh lemon juice

4 teaspoons potato starch

13

2 tablespoons (3 cl) freshly grated nutmeg

freshly ground pepper

How to prepare:

Grate the cheese. Chop the garlic and sauté in butter in the fondue pot. Add the wine, lemon juice, and cheese and cook until mixture starts to bubble. Mix the potato starch and kirsch until smooth and stir into fondue. Season with nutmeg and pepper. Bring to a boil. Transfer to tabletop burner.

To serve:

We serve this with French bread (see recipe, page 129).

Moitié-Moitié

In this recipe, Freiberg calls its fondue "half and half."

Ingredients:

10 ounces (300 g) Gruyère cheese

1 clove garlic, halved

1/3 cup (8 cl) Neuchâtel white wine

1 teaspoon fresh lemon juice

2 to 3 teaspoons cornstarch

10 ounces (300 g) Vacherin à Fondue

2 tablespoons (3 cl) kirsch

How to prepare:

Grate the Gruyère. Rub the fondue pot with garlic. Combine the cheese, wine, and lemon juice in the pot and stir over medium heat until smooth. Mix the cornstarch with a little wine and stir into cheese mixture to thicken. Grate Vacherin and add to Gruyère mixture with kirsch. Stir only until cheese is melted; do not allow to bubble.

Tip:

Do not let the fondue cook further at the table; just keep it warm.

Eastern Switzerland Fondue

This is where Vacherin à Fondue belongs.

Ingredients:

1 garlic clove, halved

8 ounces (225 g) Appenzeller cheese

8 ounces (225 g) Emmentaler cheese

1 cup (1/4 l) hard cider or apple wine

1 teaspoon fresh lemon juice

2 teaspoons cornstarch

8 ounces (225 g) Vacherin à Fondue

2 tablespoons (3 cl) kirsch

How to prepare:

Rub the fondue pot with garlic. Coarsely chop the Appenzeller and Emmentaler and combine with cider and lemon juice in the pot. Stir over medium heat until smooth. Mix the cornstarch with a little cider and stir into cheese mixture to thicken. Grate Vacherin and add to fondue mixture with kirsch. Stir only until cheese is melted; do not allow to bubble.

To serve:

Accompany with pieces of hearty peasant bread.

Geneva Fondue I

A fondue preparation which is ladled over the food rather than dipped into.

Ingredients:

1 pound (450 g) well-aged Emmentaler or Gruyère cheese

1/3 cup (8 cl) Dézaley or Vevey, Swiss white wine

1/3 cup (8 cl) heavy cream

3 egg yolks

14

freshly ground pepper

freshly grated nutmeg

How to prepare:

Depending on the age and hardness of the cheese, either chop or grate it and mix with remaining ingredients in the pot. Stir over low heat until creamy; do not allow to bubble (if the mixture boils, the egg yolks will curdle). Keep warm over a low flame.

To serve:

Ladle over toasted pieces of bread (see also recipe for Snacks, page 128) or boiled potatoes.

Geneva Fondue II

Ingredients:

1 pound (450 g) Gruyère cheese

8 ounces (225 g) Emmentaler cheese

8 ounces (225 g) Raclette mountain cheese

1½ cups (⅜ l) dry white wine

1 teaspoon fresh lemon juice

1 tablespoon potato starch

2 tablespoons (3 cl) kirsch

freshly ground pepper

½ ounce (15 g) dried mushrooms

1 tablespoon butter

How to prepare:

Prepare fondue according to the basic recipe on page 11. Soak the mushrooms in cold water for 5 minutes. Stir into finished fondue.

Variation:

Stir 2 peeled, seeded, drained and finely diced tomatoes into this fondue.

Hints:

We prefer using aromatic European dried mushrooms, not dried Chinese mushrooms, which have little aroma. As for a wine, the most appropriate is any white from the Lake Geneva area, such as Aigle, Dézaley, Dorin, Epesses, Perlan, or St. Saphorin.

15

BRANDIES FOR FONDUE

Brandy is used both as a flavoring for fondue and as a beverage to be served during the meal. According to tradition, the brandy is sipped halfway through eating the fondue; it is called, therefore, the "halfway drink" or the "drink in the middle."

Since fondue originated in Switzerland, Swiss kirsch (cherry brandy), plum brandy, and pear brandy are all appropriate. These fruit brandies are fermented without the addition of sugar and contain about 45% alcohol. (Use of the word *Wasser,* or "water," as in *Kirschwasser,* indicates that no sugar is added.) The word *Geist,* or "spirit," appears when the fruit alcohol is distilled. The marcs, usually French, are also outstanding fondue brandies. They are made from the pressings of wine grapes and have a well-rounded, full-bodied taste. The best of the marcs are Marc de Bourgogne, Marc de Champagne, Marc de Gewürztraminer and, from Switzerland, Marc de Dôle.

Grappa can also be used for flavoring fondue and for sipping with it. We recommend Grappa di Dolcetto d'Alba, which can be found in stores that stock a good selection of Italian wines.

All other brandies are for particular recipes and are used to suit individual tastes.

Gomser Fondue

This is also known as "Valais Fondue," since it is made from Gomser, a mountain cheese from the Valais region of Switzerland. If unavailable, substitute Raclette.

Ingredients:

1 pound 5 ounces (600 g) Gomser cheese

1 clove garlic, halved

1 tablespoon flour

1 tablespoon butter

2 cups (½ l) milk

freshly ground pepper

freshly grated nutmeg

How to prepare:

Shred cheese. Rub the fondue pot with garlic. Combine the flour and butter in the fondue pot and cook over medium heat until golden. Remove from heat and whisk in milk. Cook, stirring, until slightly thickened. Add cheese and stir vigorously until melted. Season to taste with pepper and nutmeg. Serve with cubed French bread.

Lucerne Fondue

The chopped herb gives a touch of color to this fondue.

Ingredients:

1 clove garlic, halved

12 ounces (360 g) Gruyère cheese

9 ounces (250 g) Appenzeller or Raclette cheese

1½ cups (⅜ l) white wine

1 teaspoon fresh lemon juice

1 tablespoon cornstarch

2 tablespoons (3 cl) kirsch

2 tablespoons chopped fresh tarragon, chervil or sage

How to prepare:

Rub fondue pot with garlic and prepare fondue according to basic recipe on page 11. Pat chopped herb dry with a paper towel and stir into fondue just before serving.

To serve:

With the bread cubes, serve bits of sausage, removed from casing, shaped into balls and cooked in boiling water.

Glarner Fondue

This fondue is made piquant with the addition of Sapsago, the green herb cheese from Switzerland.

Ingredients:

2 tablespoons butter

2 tablespoons flour

1 to 1½ cups (¼ to ⅜ l) milk

pinch salt

8 ounces (225 g) Gruyère cheese

¼ cup grated Sapsago cheese

⅓ cup (8 cl) dry white wine

freshly ground white pepper

How to prepare:

Melt butter in the fondue pot. Stir in flour. Gradually blend in milk and cook, stirring, until thick. Grate Gruyère and stir into sauce until melted. Gradually mix in Sapsago and wine. Season lightly with pepper. Keep fondue warm over a low flame.

16

Fondues are international. Here is the Italian version, Fonduta—recipe on page 25.

Ticino Fonduta

A cheese cream that is served in the mountain towns of Ticino, the Italian-speaking Swiss canton.

For the polenta:

4 cups (1 1) water

salt

9 ounces (250 g) yellow cornmeal

For the fonduta:

2 ounces (50 g) Sbrinz or Comté cheese

2 ounces (50 g) Gruyère cheese

¼ cup (50 g) butter

3 eggs

1 cup (¼ 1) milk

salt

freshly ground pepper

freshly grated nutmeg

How to prepare:

Combine water and salt in a cast iron pot and bring to a boil. Add cornmeal all at once and let stand briefly without stirring, then stir gently with a wooden spoon just enough to keep cornmeal from sticking to the bottom of the pot. Cook over very low heat until polenta is very thick and pulls away from sides of pot, about 30 minutes. Scrape polenta together and turn into a bowl.

Grate cheese. Combine all Fonduta ingredients in a fondue pot and heat slowly, stirring constantly with a wooden spoon; do not let mixture boil. When Fonduta is smooth, pour it over the polenta and serve.

Ticino Fondue

Ingredients:

8 to 10 plum tomatoes

2 cloves garlic

water or tomato juice

10 ounces (300 g) Gruyère cheese

10 ounces (300 g) Emmentaler cheese

4 teaspoons cornstarch or flour

freshly ground pepper

generous pinch dried crumbled oregano

1 tablespoon heavy cream

¼ cup (6 cl) chopped pimiento

19

How to prepare:

Peel, seed, and chop tomatoes. Mash garlic, combine with tomatoes in the fondue pot and cook over medium heat until soft. Press through a sieve into measuring cup and add water or tomato juice to make 1½ cups (⅜ 1). Remove ¼ cup of the tomato puree. Grate the cheese and add to puree remaining in pot. Mix cornstarch with reserved tomato puree until smooth. Stir into cheese mixture and cook over high heat until cheese is melted. Season with pepper and oregano. Stir in cream and pimiento and transfer to burner.

Hints:

Lazy cooks can start fondue with canned tomato puree. Ambitious cooks can use fresh roasted pimientos.

Country Fondue

Ingredients:

1 clove garlic, halved

8 ounces (225 g) Gruyère cheese

The basis for all other cheese fondues, the Neuchâtel Fondue—recipe on page 11.

8 ounces (225 g) Emmentaler cheese

8 ounces (225 g) young, sharp Raclette cheese

1 cup (¼ l) white wine

4 teaspoons potato starch

2 tablespoons (3 cl) plum brandy

freshly ground pepper

2 ounces (50 g) bacon

How to prepare:

Prepare the fondue according to the basic recipe on page 11. Dice bacon and fry until crisp. Stir bacon into fondue just before serving.

To serve:

Accompany with cubes of country bread or with Sourdough Rolls (see recipe, page 127).

Roquefort Fondue

Like Geneva Fondue I, this is spooned over its accompaniment, not used for dunking.

Picture on page 27

Ingredients:

¼ cup (50 g) butter

1 cup (¼ l) dry white wine

2 tablespoons (3 cl) Cognac

1 pound (450 g) Roquefort or other blue-veined cheese

8 ounces (225 g) Brie

½ teaspoon ground celery seed

½ teaspoon mace

freshly ground pepper

How to prepare:

Melt butter with wine and Cognac in the fondue pot. Crumble cheeses and add to pot. Heat gently until cheese melts; do not boil. Stir in seasonings. Place over candle warmer or smallest flame of a burner.

To serve:

Ladle over Blini Weisham (see recipe, page 130), French bread (page 129), or Bacon Onion Rolls (page 128), which have been sliced and arranged on plates. Eat with a knife and fork.

French Cheese Fondue

Ingredients:

8 ounces (225 g) Beaufort cheese

8 ounces (225 g) Gruyère cheese

4 ounces (100 g) Cantal cheese

2 tablespoons flour

1 clove garlic, halved

1 cup (¼ l) Chablis or Sancerre

salt

freshly ground pepper

1½ tablespoons butter

¼ cup (6 cl) heavy cream

3 tablespoons (4 cl) kirsch

How to prepare:

Dice the cheeses and shake with the flour in a plastic bag. Heat garlic in the wine in the fondue pot; discard garlic. Add cheese mixture slowly to the hot wine and stir constantly until it comes to a boil; the cheese should be completely melted before remaining ingredients are added. Stir in salt, pepper, and butter. Slowly blend the cream into the bubbling fondue, then stir in kirsch. Thin with additional warmed wine if desired.

To serve:

Dunk pieces of French bread (see recipe, page 129).

Boy Scout or Camping Fondue

Ingredients:

8 ounces (250 g) processed cheese (4 squares, 2 ounces [62.5 g] each)

1 small can button mushrooms

2 tablespoons (3 cl) kirsch

freshly ground pepper

How to prepare:

Finely chop cheese and drain mushrooms. Combine in fondue pot and place over low heat until cheese is melted. Add kirsch, season with pepper, and serve with pieces of bread.

Variation:

Leave the mushrooms whole so they can be speared with fondue forks.

Sliced Cheese Fondue

This fondue is foolproof. The slices melt easily and there is no chance of the cheese overcooking or becoming stringy.

Ingredients:

$1/2$ clove garlic or 1 onion slice

1 cup ($1/4$ l) dry white wine (Swiss, Alsatian, or Mosel-Saar-Ruwer)

9 ounces (250 g) Cheshire or Cheddar cheese slices

9 ounces (250 g) Emmentaler cheese slices

2 tablespoons (3 cl) kirsch

freshly ground white pepper

How to prepare:

Rub pot with garlic or onion. Add wine and heat slowly. Cut cheese slices into small cubes and add to wine, stirring constantly. Blend in kirsch and season with white pepper. Serve over warmer.

To serve:

Accompany with peasant bread, such as Oatmeal Bread (see recipe, page 128).

Cottage Cheese Fondue Arne

This fondue can be seasoned to taste with finely chopped fresh herbs.

Ingredients:

5 tablespoons (75 g) butter

2 pounds (1 kg) cottage cheese

2 cups ($1/2$ l) milk

1 tablespoon flour

pinch salt

pinch celery salt

3 drops Tabasco

1 teaspoon sweet paprika

4 egg yolks

How to prepare:

Melt butter in pot. Sieve cottage cheese and mix with milk until smooth. Add to butter with flour and blend well. Heat slowly, stirring constantly to prevent lumping. Mix seasonings with egg yolks and stir quickly into fondue; do not boil. Transfer to warmer.

To serve:

Use bread or celery pieces for dunking.

21

Mainzer Cheese Fondue

You can use cheese studded with caraway seeds for this fondue if you wish.

Ingredients:

1 bacon slice

1 clove garlic, halved

2 ounces (50 g) fatty bacon

1 pound 5 ounces (600 g) sour milk cheese (substitute domestic Harzer)

1 cup (¼ l) milk

1 cup (¼ l) dry white Rheinhessen wine

1 teaspoon fresh lemon juice

1 tablespoon potato starch

1 tablespoon brandy

freshly ground pepper

How to prepare:

Rub fondue pot with bacon and garlic. Chop garlic finely, dice bacon and fry in pot. Chop cheese, add to pot with milk and stir constantly until melted. Add wine and lemon juice and bring to boil. Mix potato starch and brandy and stir into bubbling fondue. Season well with pepper.

To serve:

Accompany with peasant or corn bread.

Gouda Cheese Pot

A "Kaaspott," or cheese pot, is a traditional winter dish in the Netherlands. It is nothing more than a fondue prepared with Dutch cheeses.

Ingredients:

1 clove garlic, halved

1 pound (450 g) young Gouda cheese

8 ounces (225 g) aged Gouda cheese

1 cup (¼ l) white Rhône wine or Sancerre

2 to 3 teaspoons cornstarch

1 teaspoon fresh lemon juice

freshly ground pepper

freshly grated nutmeg

2 tablespoons (3 cl) Dutch gin

How to prepare:

Rub pot with garlic. Shred young cheese and grate aged cheese. Combine in pot. Add wine and stir constantly over medium heat until mixture is melted and bubbling. Mix cornstarch and lemon juice and add to cheese mixture, thinning with more wine if desired. Season with pepper and nutmeg and stir in gin. Transfer to warmer.

To serve:

Break Dutch zwieback into pieces; cut white bread and salt sticks for dunking.

WHAT ELSE CAN BE DIPPED?

When you look in the refrigerator or frozen food case in your supermarket you will find many things that can be dipped into hot cheese. Along with bread and rolls (see page127) here are a few possibilities: apple cubes; cauliflowerets (blanched in boiling water with a little vinegar added for 3 minutes, then chilled for 30 minutes in ice cold water, drained and dusted with sweet or hot paprika); celery pieces; pickle cubes; pepper pieces; cherry tomatoes; cocktail franks; frankfurter or sausage pieces; liverwurst cubes; pieces of cooked or roasted chicken; smoked or roasted pork.

Bols Fondue

Discovered many years ago during a visit to Amsterdam.

Ingredients:

1 clove garlic, halved

1½ cups (¼ l) white Bordeaux

¼ cup (6 cl) fresh lemon juice

1 pound (450 g) Gouda cheese

freshly ground pepper

freshly grated nutmeg

4 teaspoons potato starch

2 to 4 tablespoons (3 to 6 cl) Bols cherry liqueur or kirsch

How to prepare:

Rub pot with garlic. Mix wine and lemon juice in pot and bring to boil. Grate cheese. Lower heat so wine just simmers and add cheese, stirring constantly until melted. Season with pepper and nutmeg. Mix potato starch and liqueur, stir into fondue and heat until bubbling.

To serve:

Accompany with cubes of brown bread. Drink the same red wine with the fondue.

Buttermilk Fondue

An American recipe which is perfect for teenage parties.

Ingredients:

1 pound 2 ounces (500 g) Emmentaler cheese

3 tablespoons cornstarch

½ teaspoon salt

¼ teaspoon finely ground pepper

freshly grated nutmeg

2 cups (½ l) buttermilk

1 clove garlic, halved

How to prepare:

Grate the cheese and mix with cornstarch, salt, pepper, and nutmeg. Combine buttermilk and garlic in pot and heat slowly. Discard garlic. Add the cheese mixture a handful at a time, stirring constantly until melted. Transfer to warmer.

To serve:

Use white bread cubes for dunking.

Pink Fondue

In Swiss ski huts one often encounters rosy fondues made with not-so-traditional wines.

Ingredients:

1 clove garlic, halved

1 pound 5 ounces (600 g) cheese (mixed kinds according to taste)

1 cup (¼ l) light red Swiss wine

1 teaspoon fresh lemon juice

1 tablespoon potato starch

2 tablespoons (3 cl) kirsch

freshly ground pepper

How to prepare:

Prepare according to basic recipe on page 11.

Hints:

You may want to experiment with a rosé wine. A pink fondue can also be made by adding tomato or paprika to the cheese mixture.

23

Beer Fondue

Also known as "Bavarian Fondue."

Ingredients:

1 cup (¼ l) Pilsner beer

½ cup (⅛ l) dark beer

1 pound 5 ounces (600 g) Cheshire or Cheddar cheese

1 tablespoon cornstarch

2 tablespoons (3 cl) water

1 tablespoon fresh lemon juice

freshly ground pepper

2 tablespoons (3 cl) Steinhäger or other German brandy

How to prepare:

Bring beer to boil in fondue pot, stirring constantly. Cut cheese into cubes and add to beer a handful at a time, stirring until melted. Mix cornstarch with water until smooth. Stir into cheese mixture with the lemon juice. Continue cooking until bubbly. Transfer to warmer and stir in pepper and brandy.

To serve:

Dip small pieces of rye bread or broken soda crackers into fondue.

Champagne Fondue

There are people for whom nothing is good enough, not even the usual fondues. This is for them.

Ingredients:

½ clove garlic, halved

1 pound (450 g) Emmentaler cheese

8 ounces (225 g) Gruyère cheese

1 cup (¼ l) extra dry Champagne

1 teaspoon fresh lemon juice

1 tablespoon cornstarch

freshly ground pepper

How to prepare:

Prepare fondue according to the basic recipe on page 11, substituting Champagne for white wine.

Variation:

For more pronounced Champagne flavor, prepare fondue as directed but use ⅔ cup (16 cl) white wine. When fondue is ready, stir in ⅓ cup (8 cl) bubbly, slightly warmed Champagne.

Albese Fonduta with Truffles

Some of the world's most luxurious fondues are made with truffles. Here is a classic recipe from Piedmont, the home of the white truffle.

Ingredients:

1 pound (450 g) Fontina cheese

1 cup (¼ l) milk

4 eggs

1 tablespoon butter

salt

freshly ground white pepper

1½ ounces (5 g) white truffles

How to prepare:

Chop cheese, mix with milk and let soak for 4 hours. Beat eggs. Drain cheese, discarding milk. Mix cheese with eggs and butter in the fondue pot and heat gently, stirring; the cheese should melt, but do not boil or eggs will curdle. Season with salt and pepper. When the mixture is thick and smooth, transfer to a very gentle candle warmer. Shave truffles very thinly and scatter over the top.

24

To serve:

Dunk white bread that has been cut into finger-shaped pieces, or serve with Blini Weisham (see recipe, page 130).

Hint:

Fontina can be found in Italian markets, as can the Provolone cheese used in the following recipe.

Italian Fonduta

Picture on page 17

Ingredients:

11 ounces (330 g) Provolone cheese

11 ounces (330 g) Gorgonzola cheese

1 cup (¼ l) milk

4 eggs

1 tablespoon butter

salt

freshly ground white pepper

How to prepare:

Prepare as directed in previous Fonduta recipe.

To serve:

Dunk cubes of white bread or thick mushroom slices.

Hotel Danieli Fonduta

From the opulent hotel on Venice's Grand Canal. This fonduta can also be poured on toasted slices of white bread and eaten with a knife and fork.

Ingredients:

1 pound 2 ounces (500 g) Fontina cheese

¼ cup (50 g) butter

3 egg yolks

dry white wine or light beer

salt

freshly ground white pepper

white truffles

How to prepare:

Dice Fontina and melt with butter in a pot set over simmering water. Add egg yolks and stir until mixture is a thick cream. Slowly stir in wine or beer until desired consistency. Beat until smooth. Season with salt and pepper. Place pot over a candle warmer and sprinkle generously with shredded truffle.

To serve:

Dunk cubes of white bread.

25

Fondue à la Périgueux

This fondue and the next are served with black truffles.

Ingredients:

1 clove garlic, halved

1 pound (450 g) Gruyère cheese

8 ounces (225 g) Emmentaler cheese

1 cup (¼ l) very dry white wine or Champagne

1 teaspoon fresh lemon juice

1 tablespoon cornstarch

2 tablespoons (3 cl) marc

freshly ground white pepper

2 black truffles

How to prepare:

Prepare fondue according to the basic recipe on page 11. When ready to serve, sprinkle top with thinly sliced truffles.

Note:

Marc, used here instead of kirsch, is a French *eau de vie* made from the pressings of wine grapes. Either Marc de Chablis or Marc de Bourgogne can be used.

Grand Gala Fondue à la Périgueux

Ingredients:

1 pound (450 g) Gruyère cheese

4 ounces (120 g) Vacherin à Fondue

4 ounces (120 g) Valais or Raclette cheese

1 cup (¼ l) Neuchâtel white wine

1 teaspoon fresh lemon juice

1 tablespoon cornstarch

freshly ground pepper

¼ cup (6 cl) marc (see Note above)

2 black truffles

How to prepare:

Prepare fondue according to the basic recipe on page 11. Heat marc gently. At the table, spoon it over the bubbling cheese fondue; ignite. When flames die down, sprinkle fondue with thinly sliced truffles.

Note:

Truffles can be cut with tiny cutters into a variety of decorative shapes. This makes the fondue especially festive for birthdays or holidays.

Hermitage Fondue

A special-occasion fondue for connoisseurs, prepared without any thickening.

Ingredients:

1 clove garlic, halved

1½ cups (⅜ l) dry white wine

1½ tablespoons butter

8 ounces (225 g) Valais or Raclette mountain cheese

8 ounces (225 g) Gruyère cheese

2 tablespoons (3 cl) marc (see Note, page 26)

freshly ground white pepper

How to prepare:

Rub pot heavily with the garlic. Add wine to the pot and boil until reduced by half. Add butter. Slice Valais cheese thinly; grate Gruyère. Add cheeses to wine and stir constantly until mixture bubbles. Stir in marc and pepper. Transfer to warmer and adjust heat so that fondue bubbles.

Hint:

Since this fondue is made without thickening, the stirring is very important. Use a whisk as well as the bread pieces to keep stirring the fondue at the table.

Variations on a Theme

The basic recipe for Neuchâtel Fondue (page 11) can be varied in many ways. Here are some.

Curry Fondue

How to prepare:

Add curry powder until fondue has a yellow color and is seasoned to taste.

26

Another style fondue: Roquefort Fondue is eaten from a plate and the food is not dunked—recipe on page 20.

To serve:

Spear cubes of bread with mango chutney and tiny cubes of fresh ginger and dip into fondue.

Tip:

If curry is not to your taste, substitute a small amount of saffron to get the same golden color.

Caraway Fondue

How to prepare:

For strongest flavor add 1 to 2 teaspoons caraway liqueur *(Kümmel)* to the fondue. Alternatively, Kümmel can be served separately, with each person dipping his bread into the liqueur and then into the fondue according to his own taste.

Variation:

Instead of Kümmel add ½ to 1 teaspoon ground caraway seed.

Devil's Fondue

How to prepare:

Stir 1 teaspoon Tabasco into the finished fondue at the table.

To serve:

This very spicy fondue tastes best with a strong flavored bread or with Blini Weisham (see recipe, page 130). Shrimp and lobster tails are also very good for dipping.

Fondue with Mustard

How to prepare:

Just before serving, stir either 1 tablespoon sharp prepared mustard or 1 teaspoon dry mustard into the fondue, along with 1 drop Tabasco and freshly ground pepper.

To serve:

This is good with pieces of sausage or other cold cuts for dunking.

Garlic Fondue

How to prepare:

The fondue pot should not only be rubbed with garlic, but the fondue mixture should be cooked with 3 cloves of minced garlic or the juice pressed from 3 cloves of garlic.

Fondue with Meat Sauce

How to prepare:

At the table, stir 2 tablespoons (2 cl) gravy (left over from roast or canned meat) into the fondue.

BREADS FOR FONDUE

Various breads can be served with fondue, according to personal preference. One standard choice is crisp-crusted white bread such as a French baguette, served plain or toasted. Kaiser rolls are also good, as they break easily into crusty pieces. Wheat bread is delicious, but tends to drop off the fork and get lost in the cheese. Some fondue lovers prefer a stronger-tasting rye bread, which is either cut into bite-size pieces or served in tiny loaves that the guest breaks himself. Rye rolls, salt sticks, and onion rolls are all suitable for hearty flavored cheese fondues.

Fondue bread should be at least one day old, as fresh bread is hard to spear on the fork. For further ideas see the suggestions on page 127.

Seafood is the highlight of this delicate Dill Fondue—recipe on page 31.

Tarragon Fondue

How to prepare:

Three days before the fondue is to be prepared, steep several sprigs of fresh tarragon in the wine. Discard tarragon and prepare fondue according to the basic recipe.

Mushroom Fondue I

How to prepare:

For each person, stir ¼ cup (50 g) sautéed chopped fresh mushrooms into finished fondue.

Mushroom Fondue II

How to prepare:

Pound 2 ounces (50 g) dried European mushrooms in a mortar or grind in a food processor until reduced to a fine powder. Mix with ½ teaspoon mace. Stir 1 teaspoon of the mixture into the finished fondue.

Note:

Any leftover powder is ideal for seasoning sauces and stews.

Italian Fondue

How to prepare:

Into finished fondue mix 1 tablespoon tomato paste, 1 teaspoon dried, crumbled basil, and 1 tablespoon finely diced salami.

Chive Fondue

How to prepare:

At the table, sprinkle the fondue with 1 to 2 table-spoons finely chopped fresh chives.

Olive Fondue

How to prepare:

Before serving fondue stir in 8 thinly sliced stuffed olives, 3 chopped anchovy fillets, and 1 finely chopped clove garlic.

Farmer's Garden Fondue

How to prepare:

At the table, add 2 tablespoons chopped fresh herbs (mostly parsley, with a little tarragon and mint) and 2 ounces (50 g) finely diced bacon, fried until crisp. Bacon can be sprinkled over fondue rather than mixed in, if you prefer.

Onion Fondue

Finally, a flavorful fondue that is somewhat different.

Ingredients:

1 clove garlic, halved

1 pound (450 g) Gruyère cheese

8 ounces (225 g) Emmentaler cheese

1 cup (¼ l) dry white wine

1 teaspoon fresh lemon juice or garlic vinegar

1 tablespoon cornstarch

2 tablespoons (3 cl) Cognac

freshly ground pepper

1 to 2 large onions

1 tablespoon butter

How to prepare:

Prepare fondue according to basic recipe on page 11. At the same time, mince onions and sauté in butter until soft; do not brown. Stir into hot cheese mixture and let simmer briefly.

Variations:

Add 10 finely chopped shallots to the grated cheeses as you begin preparing the fondue. *Or* fry onions in bacon fat until brown and crisp, then stir into fondue just before serving. *Or* add 2 to 3 tablespoons dehydrated onions to fondue as it cooks. *Or* add 2 tablespoons finely chopped pickled pearl onions and omit the lemon juice or vinegar.

Tip:

Along with bread, this fondue tastes particularly good with cubes of sausage, chunks of frankfurter, or Vienna sausages for dunking.

Dipped in Cheese

Here we come to the next section of cheese fondue possibilities, which expands the range of ingredients for both the fondues and the "dippers."

Meatball Fondue

We begin with the most familiar of this type.

Ingredients:

For the fondue:

Cheese fondue, basic recipe (page 11) using 1 pound (450 g) cheese

²/₃ cup (16 cl) wine

2 teaspoons cornstarch

For the meatballs:

1½ small hard rolls

5 ounces (150 g) ground beef

5 ounces (150 g) ground pork or lamb

1 onion

1 tablespoon catsup

1 egg

½ teaspoon salt

¼ teaspoon freshly ground pepper

chopped parsley

marjoram

flour or dry breadcrumbs

oil

How to prepare:

Prepare fondue according to basic recipe. For the meatballs, soak rolls in water for twenty minutes, then squeeze dry and crumble. Mix with meats. Grate the onion. Mix all ingredients, adding parsley and marjoram as desired and shaping mixture into cherry-size balls. Roll meatballs in flour or crumbs and deep fry in oil until brown and crisp. Drain on absorbent paper. Serve instead of bread for dunking.

Dill Fondue with Seafood

Picture on page 28

Ingredients:

1 pound 5 ounces (600 g) Gruyère cheese,

1 cup (¼ l) hard cider or apple wine

fresh lemon juice

1 tablespoon cornstarch

1 teaspoon kirsch

1 heaping teaspoon chopped fresh dill or 1 teaspoon dried

freshly ground white pepper

1 pound (450 g) scallops, cooked

1 pound 2 ounces (500 g) shrimp, cooked, shelled and deveined

How to prepare:

Prepare fondue according to basic recipe on page 11, using only 1 teaspoon kirsch to avoid masking the flavor of the dill. (The dill, especially if dried, should be added in the kitchen to intensify the flavor.) Cut cooked scallops into slices and sprinkle with lemon juice. Arrange them with shrimp decoratively on a platter.

To serve:

Dip scallops and shrimp into fondue, with or without cubes of bread.

31

Tips:

Shrimp, langostinos, lobster, crayfish, rock lobster tails, and mussels are all good with this fondue. Instead of kirsch, try using aquavit; its flavor is particularly compatible with dill.

Fondue à la Mode

Another fondue that tastes best with shellfish. Shrimp, lobster, langostinos, scallops, and mussels are all easy to spear.

Ingredients:

1 clove garlic, halved

1 pound (450 g) Emmentaler cheese

8 ounces (225 g) Comté cheese

1 cup (¼ l) Neuchâtel white wine

1 teaspoon fresh lemon juice

1 tablespoon cornstarch

2 teaspoons kirsch

1 tablespoon chopped fresh dill

1 teaspoon chopped fresh chervil

freshly ground pepper

How to prepare:

Prepare fondue according to basic recipe on page 11. Season and sprinkle with herbs.

To serve:

Serve with cubes of white bread, mushroom caps, and pearl onions.

Rich Fondue

Bread as well as other more colorful foods can be dipped into this mixture.

Ingredients:

½ clove garlic

1 pound (450 g) Gruyère cheese

⅔ cup (16 cl) dry white wine

1 teaspoon fresh lemon juice

1 tablespoon cornstarch

2 tablespoons (3 cl) kirsch

grappa, or gentian apéritif

freshly ground pepper

How to prepare:

Prepare fondue according to basic recipe on page 11, using grappa or gentian apéritif instead of kirsch if you wish.

To serve:

Dip toasted bread cubes as well as tiny ears of corn, stuffed olives, rolled anchovy fillets, or cubes of salami or ham.

Parmentier Fondue

Named after August Parmentier, the French pioneer in potato cultivation and the inventor of potato soup. Before selecting your potatoes, see Note to the recipe for Fondue Ranchero, page 87.

Ingredients:

Cheese fondue, basic recipe (page 11)

Kümmel (caraway liqueur)

2 tablespoons (3 cl) vodka

2 pounds (1 kg) firm cooked potatoes

How to prepare:

Flavor the fondue with desired amount of Kümmel. Stir in vodka. Peel and slice potatoes and use instead of bread for dunking.

To serve:

Cornichons and small cubes of liverwurst can accompany the potatoes.

Banana Fondue

Drink a mild rosé with this; serve with mango chutney.

Ingredients:

Cheese fondue, basic recipe (page 11), made with only Emmentaler cheese

For each person:

2 tablespoons cornflake crumbs

2 bananas

How to prepare:

Prepare fondue according to basic recipe. Cut bananas into bite-size pieces; place crumbs and bananas at each table setting. Set the fondue on the warmer. Dip banana pieces into fondue, then into crumbs.

Variation:

Instead of cornflake crumbs, serve flaked coconut for a Far Eastern touch.

Impressive Fondue

Vico Torriani invented this fondue for his European television program *Hotel Victoria*.

Ingredients:

1 clove garlic, halved

1 pound (450 g) Gruyère cheese

8 ounces (225 g) Emmentaler cheese

1 cup (¼ l) Neuchâtel white wine

1 teaspoon fresh lemon juice

1 tablespoon cornstarch

2 tablespoons (3 cl) pear brandy

freshly ground pepper

How to prepare:

Prepare fondue according to basic recipe on page 11, using pear brandy instead of kirsch.

To serve:

Peel and core juicy, ripe pears and cut into bite-size pieces. Sprinkle with lemon juice to keep them from turning brown. Spear on forks and top with bread cubes to hold fast. Dip into fondue.

Spanish Fondue

Hearty Spanish Rioja wine is particularly delicious with this fondue.

Ingredients:

Cheese fondue, basic recipe (page 11) using 1 pound (450 g) Emmentaler cheese and 8 ounces (225 g) goat cheese

For each person:

5 to 10 olives stuffed with pimiento

5 olives stuffed with almonds

5 olives stuffed with anchovies

Oatmeal Bread (see recipe, page 128)

How to prepare:

Prepare fondue according to basic recipe. Use the olives and cubes of oatmeal bread for dunking.

Tip:

Other breads, such as baguettes, can be used instead of oatmeal bread.

Pizza Fondue

In this American fondue, two dishes are combined in one: Italian pizza and Swiss fondue.

Ingredients:

1 clove garlic, halved

1 onion

4 ounces (100 g) ground beef

2 tablespoons butter

12 ounces (350 g) Fontina cheese

5 ounces (150 g) mozzarella cheese

1½ cups (⅜ l) dry white wine

1 tablespoon cornstarch

1 teaspoon fresh lemon juice

freshly ground pepper

1 teaspoon dried oregano, crumbled

How to prepare:

Rub the pot with garlic, then chop the garlic fine. Chop onion fine and sauté with garlic and beef in butter until beef is brown and crumbly. Drain excess fat. Finely dice cheeses and add to beef mixture. Add wine and slowly bring to boil, stirring constantly. Mix cornstarch and lemon juice and add to melted cheese. Stir well and season with pepper and oregano.

To serve:

Serve with lightly toasted cubes of garlic bread (see recipe, page 126) for dunking. The "halfway drink" (see page 131) should be grappa.

Mexican Fondue

This is served cold.

Ingredients:

½ cup (⅛ l) chili sauce

2 squares Gervais or one 3-ounce package cream cheese

1 tablespoon fresh lemon juice

2 teaspoons chili powder

pinch garlic powder

¼ teaspoon Tabasco

1 cup (¼ l) heavy cream

2 to 3 tablespoons (3 to 4 cl) dry Sherry

34

CUTTING AND GRATING CHEESE

For cheese to melt easily in a fondue it must be cut into small pieces—cubed, sliced thinly with a knife or cheese plane, shredded, or grated. The way it is cut will depend on the consistency and age of the cheese used. Soft or young cheeses are sliced or shredded; hard, well-aged cheeses must be grated, since they are too hard to cut and large pieces would not melt smoothly and quickly. Choose the cheeses for a fondue carefully; see "Fondue Cheeses" on page 35. Keep in mind that the more aged and ripe the cheese is, the stronger tasting will be the fondue.

All Emmentaler cheese is shredded. Appenzeller should be cubed. Edam can be sliced or shredded. Young Gouda is shredded, while aged Gouda is grated. Freiberg Vacherin is sliced or shredded. Gruyère and Sbrinz are planed or grated. Tilsiter is finely diced or shredded. Raclette is thinly sliced or shredded.

How to prepare:

Combine all ingredients and beat until smooth and well blended.

To serve:

Accompany with corn chips, cheese crackers or other cheese breads, cubes of bread, thin slices of toast, or potato chips.

Principal Fondue Cheeses

Allgäuer Emmentaler:

pale yellow hard cheese from Switzerland. Mild, nutty taste. Aged six months. Good for melting when shredded.

Appenzeller:

sharp and semi-hard, from Switzerland. Spicy aroma. Good as a second cheese in a fondue if soaked for one hour in hard cider or apple wine.

Asiago:

hard, crumbly cheese from Vicenza, Italy. Sharp, hearty taste. Grated as a seasoning cheese in fondue.

Beaufort:

hard cheese from Savoy, France. Mixed half and half with Gruyère, it makes a pungent fondue.

Bel Paese:

Italian high-fat cheese. Mild and creamy. Combine with hard cheese for better melting.

Caerphilly:

semi-soft cheese from Wales. Can be grated or shredded. Classic cheese for Welsh rarebits, which are essentially a knife-and-fork cheese fondue.

Cantal:

oldest French cheese, spicy and semi-hard. Taste before purchasing, since the flavor varies a great deal.

Cheddar:

English or American hard cheese with a crumbly texture and mild to extra-sharp taste. A popular American fondue cheese. Can be cubed easily.

Chester (Cheshire):

English hard cheese; when young has a mild taste, if aged it is sharp. Can be used without mixing with other cheeses since it melts very easily.

Comté:

French hard cheese, similar to Gruyère.

Danbo:

slicing cheese from Denmark, sometimes made with caraway seed. Can be used as a second cheese in fondue.

Edam:

mild slicing cheese from Holland, sold coated with red paraffin in a ball shape. Young cheese is mild, and good for fondue alone or mixed with other cheeses.

Emmentaler:

hard Swiss cheese with large holes. Mild taste, delicate hazelnut flavor; when well aged with drops of salt water in the holes, has a sharp taste. Mixed with Gruyère in the traditional fondue.

Fontina:

high-fat Italian cheese with a delicate aroma and sweet taste. Melts in the mouth. Used as the base of the Italian fondue, the *fonduta*.

Gjetost:

sweet Norwegian hard cheese. Made from cow's and goat's milk. Color is an orangy dark brown. It is sliced with a cheese plane, has a caramelized taste and is interesting when used to season a fondue.

Gouda:

high-fat slicing cheese from Holland. It is sold in three grades of aging—1. Young Gouda, creamy, tangy, mild and soft, five to eight weeks old. Melts

35

easily and combines well with other ingredients. 2. Partially-aged Gouda, hearty, sharp and firmer, two to six months old. Also melts easily. 3. Aged Gouda, very hearty and sharp, older than six months. Easily grated and should be used as a seasoning cheese in a mixture of cheeses for fondue.

Gruyère:

closely related to Emmentaler. A hard cheese from western Switzerland with a few pea-sized holes. Cracks in the cheese indicate good quality. Spicier and sharper in taste than Emmentaler. *the* fondue cheese.

Havarti:

Danish version of Tilsiter, semi-hard with large and small holes. Has a delicate, tangy taste. Gives fondue outstanding flavor.

Mozzarella:

white, lightly tangy soft cheese from Italy, perfect for pizza. For a fondue it should be melted with milk. It does not tolerate wine; must be heated very gently.

Parmesan:

low-fat hard cheese from Italy with a dark rind. Has a crumbly, scaly texture when broken. Spicy and melts in the mouth. Grated into fondue, it gives an outstanding, different taste.

Pecorino:

sharp Italian cheese that looks like a small Parmesan. Piquant taste. Use grated as a seasoning cheese in fondue.

Provolone:

Italian slicing cheese; golden brown rind and pale yellow color inside. Young cheese tastes sweet and buttery; aged, the taste ranges from piquant to sharp. In a fondue it should be mixed with Gruyère or Emmentaler.

Samsoe:

slicing cheese from Denmark. Has large holes and a nutty taste. Young Samsoe is mild; aged, it becomes sharper. It melts easily and can be used instead of Emmentaler in fondues.

Sapsago:

hard, low-fat cheese from Glarus in Switzerland. It is green in color, the result of adding sage and other herbs to the cheese. Spicy, unmistakable aroma. Used grated as seasoning in fondues, and important in Glarner Fondue.

Sbrinz:

hard cheese from central Switzerland, aged two to three years. Very few pinhole-size holes. As a seasoning cheese in fondue it is planed or grated. When melted it never forms strings. When unavailable, substitute Comté.

Tilsiter:

hard slicing cheese with a golden color and tiny holes. The most familiar German cheese. Light tangy taste. Aged Tilsiter is outstanding for a spicy fondue. It does not have to be mixed with other cheeses.

Vacherin à Fondue:

not to be confused with the flat, round, high-fat cheese of the same name, which is sold in the winter months in thin wooden boxes. Vacherin à Fondue (also called Freiberg Vacherin) is much thicker and is aged only three months. It is used for Freiberger Fondue. Vacherin must not be allowed to boil.

Valais (Gomser, Bagnes):

cheese from the high Alps in Switzerland. High-fat and soft to cut. The aroma is fresh, rich and creamy. It is the ideal melting cheese (see recipe, page 16) but can also be used for fondue. When unavailable, substitute Raclette.

Velveeta:

the trade name of a melting cheese. It can be used plain or with other cheeses to make a fondue suitable for children.

Raclette

To close the section on cheese, we choose a beautiful, sociable meal: raclette. It is the original of all melted cheese dishes in Switzerland. In one of Johanna Spyri's *Heidi* books there is a description of

Raclette forms a beautiful meal. Here it is being melted in individual pans—recipe on page 39.

a rustic raclette preparation: *"The old man sat on a round wooden stool and lit a bright fire. . . . He held a large piece of cheese speared on a long iron fork and turned it back and forth until it was golden brown on all sides. Then he came to the table with the broiled cheese and placed it on a piece of bread. The child bit into the bread spread with the cheese, which during the broiling had become soft as butter, and they tasted wonderful together."*

In the Valais, the Swiss canton where raclette is a specialty, a cheese is cut crosswise into two halves. The cut side is held next to a wood fire until the surface melts. Plates, so hot that they must be handled with a cloth, are waiting, and at the right moment (through practice one learns just when) the melted layer of cheese is scraped with a special scraper or large knife onto the plate. Two peeled boiled potatoes, two pearl onions, and a cornichon or piece of pickle are served with the cheese, which must be eaten immediately.

There are special raclette broilers available in some gourmet shops. They cook anywhere from one to two portions all the way to a half wheel of cheese.

Raclette

Picture on page 37

Ingredients:

Raclette cheese

boiled potatoes

pickled pearl onions

pickles

salt

freshly ground pepper

How to prepare:

It is important that the cheese have a large cut surface. If you have a fireplace, hold the cut side of the cheese before the fire with a metal fork. As the surface melts, scrape it off with a knife onto small individual plates. The host will not have time to eat if he prepares all the raclette; therefore, when the first guest has eaten, the cooking should be rotated among the diners.

Important:

Plates must be hot and the portions of cheese small, so that the cheese will not cool too rapidly and toughen.

To serve:

Accompany with the potatoes and condiments. A full-flavored red is the best wine—particularly Dôle, which, like the raclette itself, is from the Valais.

39

Hint:

Raclette cheese is best for this recipe, as its high fat content makes it easy to melt and it remains creamy. If you cannot find Raclette cheese, substitute a high-fat solid cheese like Tilsiter or Gruyère.

Tip:

If you have no fireplace and no special raclette cooker, arrange portion-size pieces of cheese in small Teflon-coated pans and place over low heat to melt. Alternatively, butter heatproof plates, place thick slices of cheese on them and melt in the oven or under the broiler.

It is possible also to fry cheese in oil, making a Cheese Fondue Bourguignonne—recipe on page 43.

FAST AND FRESH

Meats and Seafoods
Quick-Fried in Oil

The most familiar oil-dipped fondue is Fondue Bourguignonne; if this word is too hard, call it Meat Fondue. The only thing it has in common with cheese fondues is that it is a sociable meal with the food cooked in one pot. It is more than a pot of fat that wandered to the table, since the guests, not the host, do the cooking.

This mode of eating has a long history in the Japanese fondue called *tempura.* In the seventeenth century the Portuguese were the first Europeans to come to Japan, along with the Jesuits who wanted to convert the Japanese to Christianity. Though the Europeans were expelled from the country in 1638, the Japanese had in the meantime adopted the intruders' practice of cooking in deep fat. The recipes were adjusted to Japanese taste with use of a lighter batter and a lighter oil, but the name of the dish was retained. Latin in origin, the word "tempura" means "time," or more exactly, "fasting time," during which one eats shrimp and other seafood fried in batter.

The Burgundian Fondue is much younger, having originated only in the 1950s. It was probably the discovery of a Swiss gourmet who gathered his guests around the oil pot instead of the cheese pot. The first time the recipe was printed—in *Annabelle,* the major Swiss women's magazine—it went under the adventurous name of "Mormo the Turk."

Perhaps the recipe became so beloved all over the world because not even the worst cook can spoil it, as long as the oil is fresh and the meat is of good quality. The procedure must be explained in detail.

Basic Recipe

Fondue Bourguignonne

Picture on page 48

Ingredients:

1½ to 2 pounds (600 to 800 g) beef filet, sirloin, or round steaks

4 cups (1 l) vegetable oil

How to prepare:

The meat should be tender and have fat and sinews removed; if you can find aged beef, so much the better. For the most flavorful and tender results, the day before serving cut the meat into ¾-inch cubes and dip them into olive oil. Line a shallow dish with onion slices and arrange the meat on top. Season with coarsely ground pepper (try lemon pepper), salt, and marjoram, and top with more onion slices. Cover the bowl with foil or plastic wrap and refrigerate for 12 to 24 hours.

On the day of the party, drain the meat cubes and arrange on a large board or on small individual boards.

Very important:

The meat must be well drained, as any drops of liquid will make the oil spatter.

The Oil Pot and Other Equipment

The pot for the oil should be made of copper, steel or enameled cast iron. Do not use a pot made of clay or glazed ceramic; if oil gets into the pores of unglazed clay it becomes rancid after a time, and a ceramic pot is not made to withstand the high temperature of the oil (400° F or 200° C). If such a pot breaks on the burner you will have serious trouble. If you do not want to purchase a special vessel, any heavy pot can be substituted, though it will not be as pretty.

Most oil fondue pots are narrower at the top than the bottom, to keep the fat from splattering. There is a metal collar that can be placed on top of the pot to catch splashes; it also has slits to hold the forks.

The fat should only fill the pot halfway. It is heated in the kitchen until it reaches the smoking point—that is, the moment the fat becomes still and starts to smoke. Then the pot is transferred to the tabletop burner. Use a flavorless, odorless oil; do not use olive oil. We have no use for mixtures of different fats, since they are inclined to splatter, and butter and margarine contain too much water and have much lower smoking points. Do not let the used fat from a fondue stand for too long before using it in other ways in the kitchen. If you prepare a meat fondue every week, the fat can be used four to six times.

The picks can be made of wood, since they do not burn the mouth, but they quickly take on a burned look. You can also use long-tined fondue forks with heatproof handles; do not buy cheap forks or the handles may melt. There are special forks with hooks on the handles, to suspend from the rim of the pot. Others have small barbs on the tines to keep the meat from falling off into the oil—there is no fun connected with this as for cheese fondues, where lost bread is rewarded with a kiss. It is only a nuisance, since the meat can burn easily and it is no fun to fish it out of the oil.

In any case, each guest should have two skewers: one for cooking and one for eating. A metal fork on which the meat is cooked in a fat pot is so hot it can give second-degree burns to the lips. The ritual is simple: Everyone cooks his meat rare or well done, according to his own taste. While the piece of meat is eaten, the next piece is placed in the pot. In this way, not too many forks or skewers stand or hang in the boiling oil, lowering the temperature. Knowledgeable guests pause for a drink before adding the next piece of meat to allow the oil to return to the proper temperature.

After frying, each diner seasons his own piece of meat with salt, pepper, sweet paprika, and/or chili powder. The hot meat readily absorbs the seasonings. Small bowls of cornichons, black and green olives, shredded celery, finely chopped onion, pearl onions, ground peanuts, cranberries, sliced or whole radishes, freshly grated horseradish, pimiento, hot peppers, pickled pears, mixed pickles, mustard pickles, chutneys and relishes are all good accompaniments.

Don't be alarmed; you need not buy out all the stock of a delicatessen when you prepare a meat fondue. Pick out a few according to these guidelines: something sharp, something sweet-sour, something fresh, something mild, something crisp. In time, if you are a fondue fan, you can assemble a collection of condiments—especially good are those that are homemade.

Slicing Meats for a Fondue

In Switzerland there are butchers who specialize in fondue meat. They freeze the meat before slicing, then cut it paper-thin on a slicing machine. Paper is placed between the thin slices to make them easier to separate.

Do it the same way at home. The meat—the best is filet or sirloin—should be frozen until firm but not rock hard. Then cut paper-thin with a sharp knife. Alternatively, buy frozen meat at your market (or take it from your own freezer), let it thaw some-what, and slice.

Look for a butcher who will slice meat for fon-due. It is important to have the right piece of meat sliced and packed properly, so it can be separated easily into good-looking slices. Butchers who sell prosciutto are accustomed to placing pieces of paper between slices.

Sauces and Dips

Here we come to the essential packaged sauces: many varieties of ketchup, chili sauce, Tabasco, steak sauce, mustard, horseradish. These are only possibilities; the choice is great.

The most important are those sauces and dips that are homemade; they can be the sensation of the fondue. We have tried many, which you will find on pages 104 to 122. There are over 50 sauces here that you can make in style.

The rules for drinks are not as stringent as with cheese fondues. We serve red wine, rosé, or beer. If you love white wine, drink it; but it should be hearty in flavor.

A Recipe Sampler

New Zealand Lamb Fondue

Ingredients:

2 pounds (1 kg) New Zealand lamb cutlets

about 3 cups (¾ l) vegetable oil

How to prepare:

Cut meat into small, thin slices. Heat oil. Arrange individual portions of meat on a board or plate in front of each person.

To serve:

Accompany with garlic bread (see recipe, page 126).

Frikadellen Fondue

The most highly prized meat fondue is made with ground meat. Here is a German version.

Ingredients:

12 ounces (350 g) boneless lean beef

5 ounces (150 g) boneless pork

1 egg yolk

4 to 5 tablespoons fine dry breadcrumbs

2 drops Tabasco

1 tablespoon chopped parsley

salt

freshly ground pepper

lettuce leaves

about 3 cups (¾ l) oil

How to prepare:

Grind meats several times with the fine blade of a grinder or in a food processor. Mix meats with egg yolks, crumbs, Tabasco, parsley, salt, and pepper. Shape mixture into ¾-inch balls and chill for 1 hour. Arrange meatballs on lettuce leaves before each guest.

Caribbean Meatballs

We ate this meatball fondue in Jamaica.

Ingredients:

1 pound (450 g) cooked skinned chicken

1 egg

2 tablespoons finely chopped parsley

1 tablespoon grated onion

1 teaspoon curry powder

salt

42

1 teaspoon dry mustard

fine dry breadcrumbs

about 3 cups (¾ l) oil

For each person:

1 beaten egg white

2 to 3 tablespoons finely crushed zwieback

How to prepare:

Mince chicken and beat egg. Combine both with remaining ingredients (except oil) to form a thick mixture. Shape into walnut-size pieces and chill for 1 hour. Heat the oil in the fondue pot. Before each guest place small bowls holding beaten egg white and crumbs. Spear meatballs on forks, dip them first into egg white and then into crumbs, and fry for 1 minute.

Tip:

This fondue is best served outdoors to allow the smoke from the zwieback crumbs to dissipate.

Variations:

Into the chicken mix 1 ounce (30 g) flaked coconut or finely diced ham or tiny cubes of hard cheese.

Cheese Fondue Bourguignonne

Picture on page 38
This is both a cheese and an oil fondue.

Ingredients:

1¾ pounds (800 g) high-fat cheese such as Bonbel or Bel Paese

2 eggs

1 cup (100 g) fine dry breadcrumbs

salt

freshly ground pepper

flour

4 cups (1 l) oil

How to prepare:

Dice cheese. Beat eggs. Season breadcrumbs with salt and pepper. Coat cheese cubes lightly with flour, then dip in egg and coat with seasoned crumbs. Let stand at room temperature for 1 hour. Heat the oil, dip in cheese cubes and cook for 1 minute.

To serve:

Serve with a chicory salad.

Hints:

The cheese must be dipped carefully so that it does not drip out of the breading. Since the oil tends to spatter when the cheese is dunked, you should use a fondue pot with a spatter guard.

Bolivian Cheese

At the Monk's Inn on Manhattan's West Side we ate a fondue that comes from Bolivia. The Bolivian goat cheese *Queso di Cabra* is most suitable; if you cannot find it, substitute a French, Italian, or Bulgarian goat cheese.

Ingredients:

1 pound (450 g) goat cheese

flour

4 cups (1 l) oil

sweet paprika

hot paprika

How to prepare:

Mix cheese with enough flour to make a mixture thick enough to shape into walnut-size balls. Roll balls in flour. Fry in hot oil until crusty and brown. Season with both paprikas.

43

More Meat and Poultry Dips

Chicken Fondue Bourguignonne

Ingredients:

8 chicken breasts

2 tablespoons (3 cl) olive oil

2 tablespoons (3 cl) wine vinegar

rosemary

thyme

4 green bell peppers

cocktail onions

mushroom caps

salt

freshly ground pepper

4 cups (1 l) oil

How to prepare:

Cut the skinned and boned chicken breasts into thin strips and marinate in a mixture of oil, vinegar, and herbs. Drain and pat dry with paper towels. Stem and seed peppers and cut into squares. Arrange chicken, peppers, onions and mushrooms decoratively on serving plates. Spear chicken and vegetables and fry in hot oil.

To serve:

This is especially good with saffron rice.

Lamb Fondue, Syrian Style

Ingredients

2 pounds (1 kg) dried apricots

1 teaspoon lemon pepper

¼ cup (6 cl) apricot brandy

4 cups (1 l) water

2 pounds (1 kg) boneless lamb

4 cups (1 l) oil

How to prepare:

Mix apricots, pepper, brandy and water and let stand overnight. Drain apricots, reserving syrup. Cut lamb into cubes or chunks. Marinate lamb in reserved apricot liquid.

Refrigerate apricots until serving time. Remove meat from marinade and pat dry with paper towels. Arrange decoratively on plates.

Spear first an apricot, then a piece of meat on a fork and fry together in hot oil.

Tips:

The fruit can be wrapped in thin slices of lamb and then cooked. Use the leftover apricots to prepare Chutney (see recipe, page 123).

Korean Chicken

Ingredients:

1 pound 5 ounces (600 g) boned and skinned chicken

2 onions

1 clove garlic

5 tablespoons (8 cl) soy sauce

1 tablespoon sugar

2 tablespoons (3 cl) oil (preferably sesame oil)

44

freshly ground pepper

1 tablespoon cornstarch

vegetable oil

sesame seed

How to prepare:

Cut chicken into strips or cubes. Chop onions. Mash garlic. Combine all ingredients except sesame seed, adding enough vegetable oil to cover. Marinate chicken for at least 1 hour, or overnight in refrigerator. Drain chicken well, reserving marinade. Spear on fondue forks or wooden skewers and fry in hot oil.

Heat marinade, adding sesame seed. Place in small bowls in front of each guest. Dip the cooked chicken pieces into the marinade after cooking.

Fried Liver Packets

Ingredients:

1 pound (450 g) chicken livers

1 tablespoon butter

1 can (4 ounces) water chestnuts

8 ounces (225 g) sliced bacon

salt

freshly ground pepper

ground ginger

3 cups (¾ l) oil

How to prepare:

Cut livers into bite-size pieces and sauté in butter for 10 minutes. Cool. Drain water chestnuts and cut into pieces. Halve bacon slices crosswise and wrap 1 piece of liver and 1 piece of water chestnut in each half slice. Season with salt, pepper and ginger. Spear on forks and fry in hot oil until bacon is crisp and brown.

Variation:

Warm the water chestnuts in their liquid. Place the chestnuts and pieces of sautéed liver in a partially cooked Blini (see recipe, page 130) and wrap to enclose. Fry in hot fat until brown.

Asian Fondue

Ingredients:

1 pound (450 g) boneless tender beef

1 can bamboo shoots

5 tablespoons (8 cl) soy sauce

2 tablespoons (3 cl) dry Sherry

few drops Tabasco

2 pounds (1 kg) vegetable shortening

How to prepare:

Cut the beef into paper-thin slices. Cut the bamboo shoots into matchstick pieces. Marinate bamboo shoots in soy sauce mixed with Sherry for 1 to 2 hours. Brush the beef with Tabasco, top with 2 or 3 pieces of bamboo shoot and roll up. Spear on fork and cook in hot shortening until brown.

Hints:

This is best with large beef slices; serve with a knife and fork. Spicy sauces make good accompaniments.

Mongolian Meat Pot

A version of the famous Mongolian Hot Pot.

Ingredients:

1 pound (450 g) boneless tender beef

¼ cup (6 cl) soy sauce

2 tablespoons (3 cl) Sherry or rice wine

45

1 tablespoon sugar

1 can bamboo shoots

1 piece fresh ginger

8 ounces (225 g) fresh mushrooms

2 to 4 small carrots

2 cups (½ l) oil

1 pound (450 g) butter

4 egg yolks

How to prepare:

Marinate the thinly sliced beef in soy sauce, Sherry, and sugar for 1 hour. Slice the bamboo shoots, ginger and mushrooms; cut carrots into thin lengthwise slices. Drain beef; arrange with vegetables on a large platter.

Heat the oil and butter in a large skillet or in a fondue pot, but not as hot as for a regular meat fondue. Fry beef and vegetables until tender (speared on forks or not, as you prefer). Place a bowl with 1 beaten egg yolk at each place setting. Dip every bite into egg before eating—this tastes good and cools the food.

Venison Fondue

Game is also correct for a fondue, and it gives meat fondues a whole new taste. We like it cooked in vegetable shortening instead of oil.

Ingredients:

2 pounds (1 kg) venison leg or rib

4 cups (1 l) dry red wine

1 onion

2 tablespoons pickling spice

crumbled rosemary

4 cups (1 l) vegetable shortening or oil

How to prepare:

Remove skin and sinews from meat and marinate 2 to 3 days in red wine, chopped onion and pickling spice; if the wine does not entirely cover the meat add water as necessary. Remove meat, drain thoroughly and cut into thin slices. Dust with rosemary, then spear and fry briefly in hot fat.

To serve:

Good with Apricot Chutney and Cranberry Horseradish (see recipes, pages 123 and 120).

Venison Rack Fondue

A somewhat expensive but very tasty fondue. The "feel" of the meat tells when it is cooked.

Ingredients:

1 pound 5 ounces (600 g) boneless rack of venison

2 large, firm pears

lemon pepper

1½ pounds (700 g) vegetable shortening

How to prepare:

Freeze venison until firm, then slice thinly. Peel and core pears, cut into thin slices and drain well on paper towels. Season meat and pears with lemon pepper. Arrange decoratively on plates. Wrap pieces of pear in venison, spear on forks and fry quickly in hot shortening.

To serve:

Good with Cranberry Horseradish (see recipe, page 120) and spicy prepared remoulade sauce.

Simple Game Fondue

Venison and reindeer meat are highly prized, but any game makes a good, quick fondue.

46

Fish Fondue is a satisfying dish, a refreshing change—recipe on page 54.

Ingredients:

2 pounds (1 kg) boneless game

1 cup (¼ l) white wine vinegar

2 cups (½ l) water

6 juniper berries

1 tablespoon Düsseldorf mustard

12 ounces (350 g) pitted sour cherries

5 ounces (150 g) bacon

2 pounds (1 kg) vegetable shortening

How to prepare:

Cut game into bite-size pieces. Marinate in a mixture of vinegar, water, mashed juniper berries and mustard for 1 day. Drain and pat dry. Drain cherries. Cut bacon into pieces the same size as the pieces of game. Arrange the game and bacon on a platter. Serve the cherries in a bowl. Spear game, then cherry, then bacon on a fork and fry all in hot shortening until the bacon is crisp.

Ham Toast Fondue

It takes time to prepare this, but the taste is worth it.

Ingredients:

1 loaf unsliced firm white bread, one day old

1 pound 10 ounces (750 g) vegetable shortening

3 cups (¾ l) oil

For each person:

2 tablespoons butter

3 ounces (75 g) cooked ham

2 ounces (50 g) Emmentaler or other flavorful cheese

olives

How to prepare:

Cut the bread into thin slices. For each person, toast 4 slices of bread on one side. Spread the toasted side with butter. Grind or mince ham. Grate cheese. Spread the ham thickly on two of the buttered slices and top with the cheese. Top with remaining toast slices, buttered side down, and press with a weight for 30 minutes. Cut each sandwich into 8 pieces. Spear and fry in hot fat until brown. Spear an olive on top before eating.

Sausage Fondue

Easy and fun to serve with sauces (see page 104) and beer. We prefer to cook everything in vegetable shortening instead of oil.

Ingredients:

2 pounds (1 kg) bologna or mortadella

10 bratwurst

1 pound 5 ounces (600 g) kielbasa

1 pound (450 g) unsliced boiled ham

8 frankfurters

1 pound (450 g) cocktail franks

1 pound 5 ounces (600 g) assorted cold cuts

10 smoked links or any other desired sausages

How to prepare:

Half fill the pot with fat and set over the burner. Give every guest one plate and two forks (remember, one fork for cooking, one for eating). Accompany with a basket of bread, prepared sauces in bowls for dunking, mustard, some freshly chopped herbs, pickles, and pickled onions.

Note:

Cut everything into bite-size pieces. Pre-cooked meats will cook quickly; raw sausages will take longer.

49

With different sauces, you can add variety of the classic Fondue Bourguignonne—recipe on page 40.

Seafood Fondues

From meat to fish. Though most of the classic fish fondues are prepared with broth (these will be considered in the next chapter), there are a few oil fondues made with fish and seafood.

The oil for seafood fondues is sometimes perfumed with garlic. To do this, spear 2 or 3 cloves garlic on wooden skewers and fry in the oil just until they begin to brown, then remove and discard garlic.

Ingredients:

8 ounces (225 g) cleaned squid

1 pound (450 g) cooked, shelled and deveined shrimp or langostinos

8 ounces (225 g) shelled fresh or frozen mussels

oil

How to prepare:

Cut squid into bite-size pieces. Drain the seafood well and pat dry to keep the fat from spattering. Arrange attractively on a platter. Spear and fry in hot oil.

To serve:

Serve with a variety of sauces and steamed rice. And don't forget to have some fresh or dried dill on the table.

Fish Kabob Fondue

Ingredients:

1 large package frozen fish sticks (16 pieces)

2 cups (½ l) vegetable or peanut oil

How to prepare:

Cut each fish stick into 3 pieces. Place on a platter. Heat oil, spear pieces on a fork and fry until brown, about 2 minutes.

To serve:

Have a variety of sauces.

California Shrimp Fondue

Ingredients:

½ cup (110 g) butter

1 tablespoon fresh lemon juice

lemon pepper

1 pound 10 ounces (750 g) cooked, shelled and deveined shrimp

12 halved artichoke hearts (canned)

3 cups (¾ l) vegetable oil

50

OILS AND FATS FOR FONDUE

This type of fondue uses an oil that is tasteless and odorless; olive oil is not appropriate. Suitable vegetable fats or shortenings have a high smoking point.

The fat is heated in the fondue pot in the kitchen to the point where it becomes still; the fat should only fill the pot halfway. Then it is carried to the table, placed on the burner and kept at 375° F (180° C).

Vegetable oil can be flavored by frying small cubes of partially cooked smoked bacon in it; never put fresh, uncooked bacon into hot fat, as it may explode. (All foods to be cooked should be patted dry to prevent spattering.) If you wish to flavor the oil with garlic, place 2 or 3 cloves into the oil and fry until they are light brown, then remove.

Also remember that bread cubes fried in hot fat are delicious.

How to prepare:

Mash the butter with lemon juice and lemon pepper. Alternate dipping and frying the shrimp and the artichokes until they just turn brown. Dip into butter mixture.

To serve:

Serve with pieces of French bread that are fried in the oil in between the shrimp and artichokes.

Shrimp in Packets

Can be served alone, or added to any oil fondue made with seafood.

Ingredients:

1 pound (450 g) cooked, shelled and deveined shrimp

minced fresh dill

pepper

1 can (1 pound 5 ounces) pineapple chunks

8 ounces (225 g) bacon

3 cups (¾ l) oil

How to prepare:

Season shrimp with dill and pepper. For each packet wrap 1 shrimp and 1 pineapple chunk (well drained on paper towels) in a piece of bacon. Spear on fork and fry in hot oil until the bacon is crisp.

Variation:

Instead of wrapping in bacon, wrap in Blini (see recipe, page 130).

Strausak Seafood Fondue

We received this unusual recipe from a reader in Switzerland. It takes some work to prepare, but we want to present it to you.

Ingredients:

For each person:

1 pound (450 g) squid, shrimp, lobster, clams, or other seafood

about 1 pound (450 g) spinach

lettuce leaves

fresh sage leaves

4 cups (1 l) oil

How to prepare:

Clean the seafood and cut into 1-inch cubes. Wash the spinach, lettuce and sage leaves and rinse with boiling water. Wrap the fish pieces in the leaves. Spear each packet on a wooden skewer and arrange on a platter (with green coats they are pretty). Fry packets in hot oil.

51

To serve:

On the table have ketchup mixed with a few drops of Cognac, a light garlic mayonnaise, and soy sauce. Serve each guest a small bowl of cooked rice sprinkled with a few drops of Vietnamese fish sauce (found in Oriental markets).

Japanese Oil Fondues

We have already mentioned the origin of the Japanese oil fondue, tempura (see page 52). This dish is the pride of the Japanese kitchen and has made enthusiastic fans of us. Tempura can be made quickly out of many foods—fish, seafood, meat, vegetables, any foods with a high water content.

The Japanese mix many varieties of oil. This does not suit our tastes; we prefer peanut oil to which ⅕ sesame oil is added. The temperature of the oil should remain at 350° F (175° C) all during the cooking, so we like to prepare tempura in an electric frypan or electric fondue pot (see page 133). The batter should be cold and thin. The pieces of shrimp, vegetables or meat are dipped into the batter and placed in the hot oil. Instantly cold and hot meet: The dough puffs up (be careful, as it can spatter) and the inside is cooked as the moisture in the food turns to steam. In tempura restaurants the food is served right from the pot; we do the same.

Important:

After frying, remove all the tiny pieces of fried dough from the oil with a small sieve or slotted spoon, so they don't burn and cause odors. The fewer the pieces fried at one time, the better they are, because the oil temperature remains constant.

Tempura

Two well-known tempura schools in Japan disagree on whether to add a pinch of salt to the batter, each contending that the result is crispier their way. We have chosen the salt-free cooking method.

Ingredients:

1 eggplant

flour

2 leeks

8 mushrooms

4 water chestnuts

5 ounces (150 g) raw mackerel fillets

10 ounces (300 g) shrimp or langostinos

8 ounces (225 g) raw mussels

4 cups (1 l) oil

For the batter:

1 egg yolk

2 cups (½ l) ice water

pinch of baking soda

2¼ cups (250 g) all-purpose flour

How to prepare:

Halve eggplant lengthwise. Peel one or both halves. Cut into thin slices. Coat slices in flour. Cut leeks diagonally into ½-inch pieces. Halve the mushrooms and cut the water chestnuts into cubes. Cut the mackerel fillets into cubes and coat mackerel and shrimp with flour. Shell mussels (this is easier if you drop them into lightly salted boiling water for 1 minute).

For the batter, beat egg yolk with water and baking soda, add flour and beat with a spoon until smooth.

The batter should be prepared when the guests are at the table and the oil is hot; it should flow easily from the spoon. Dip the foods into the batter (this is most easily done by spearing the food on skewers). Remove, drain and place into hot oil. Fry 2 minutes. Drain on a board covered with paper towels and have guests help themselves to finished tempura.

To serve:

Each guest should have a bowl of tempura sauce for dipping. Here are three possibilities:

Tempura Sauce I

Ingredients:

3 parts fish broth

1 part Sherry or mirin (sweet rice wine)

1 part Japanese soy sauce

1 teaspoon monosodium glutamate

1 part grated onion or grated fresh ginger

How to prepare:

Prepare the fish broth with fish trimmings, shrimp shells, and the like; do not add salt or any other seasoning. Mix broth with wine and soy sauce. Add MSG and bring to boil. Pour over onion or ginger and let stand until cooled. Serve at room temperature.

Tempura Sauce II

Ingredients:

1 tablespoon salt

1 tablespoon monosodium glutamate

3 tablespoons (4 cl) fresh lemon juice

How to prepare:

Combine all ingredients and stir well. Serve this piquant paste on a plate.

Tempura Sauce III

Ingredients:

4½ tablespoons (7 cl) Japanese soy sauce

½ cup (⅛ l) clear beef broth

2 tablespoons sugar

1 teaspoon monosodium glutamate

How to prepare:

Stir the soy sauce into the hot broth along with sugar and MSG. Dip the tempura into this "Tientsin Sauce."

Mushroom Tempura

An American invention.

Ingredients:

1 pound (450 g) mushrooms

fresh lemon juice

4 cups (1 l) oil

For the batter:

1 cup (100 g) all-purpose flour

pinch of salt

1 egg

⅓ cup (8 cl) milk

How to prepare:

Clean the mushrooms and halve if large. Rub with lemon juice. For the batter, sift the flour and salt together. Beat egg, add with milk to flour and beat to a smooth batter. Heat oil. Spear mushrooms on fondue forks, dip into the batter, drain off excess and fry until golden brown.

To serve:

Serve with a mixture of mustard and soy sauce.

You can make dozens of tempuras depending on the meat, fish, or vegetables available. Some of our particular favorites are squid, ham, and banana cubes, rolled anchovies, lightly cooked cauliflowerets, and raw pieces of asparagus.

53

WHICH FISH FOR A FISH FONDUE?

You may have noticed that when you use certain fish, such as trout, for a fondue your fork comes out of the oil without the fish, because it falls apart easily. It is best to fry or broil such fish in one large piece. Among the fish best suited to cutting into the small pieces needed for a fondue are: eel, halibut, fresh tuna, haddock, swordfish, mullet, turbot, snapper, scrod, and cod. Appropriate shellfish include shrimp, lobster, crabs, spiny lobster tails, and crayfish, as well as mussels, scallops, clams, oysters, and pieces of precooked abalone. Norwegian fish balls can also be fried in oil; they can be purchased in cans or prepared at home according to the recipe on page 125. Frozen fish sticks and fish balls can be fried, as can squid and octopus. **Hint:** Marinating fish in fresh lemon juice will improve the flavor.

Other Favorite Oil-Cooked Fondues

Between Tempura and Fondue Bourguignonne is:

German Fish Fondue

A summer fondue that is well suited to alfresco dining.
Picture on page 47

Ingredients:

2 pounds (1 kg) red snapper fillet

salt

juice of 2 lemons

pinch of saffron

4 cups (1 l) oil

For the batter:

2¼ cups (250 g) all-purpose flour

½ cup (⅛ l) beer

3 tablespoons grated cheese

3 tablespoons (4 cl) oil

How to prepare:

Cut the fish into cubes (not too small) and marinate in salt, lemon juice and saffron for 1 hour. Prepare the batter with half of the flour beaten with the beer. Stir in cheese and slowly stir in the oil (the batter should be creamy and thick but flowing; if not, gradually stir in more beer). Heat the oil in the pot. Spear the fish on forks, coat pieces with remaining flour and then with batter. Drain and fry in hot oil until golden.

Valais Fish Fondue

The Swiss cook Charly Launer created Fondue Matterhorn in the summer of 1966. A variation of tempura, it consists of fish pieces, shrimp and scallops that are dipped in batter and fried in oil. We don't have his recipe, but here's a very similar one.

Ingredients:

8 ounces (225 g) frozen flounder fillets

1 pound 10 ounces (750 g) haddock fillets

8 ounces (225 g) halibut

1 tablespoon flour

2 egg whites

1 teaspoon sweet paprika

salt

½ teaspoon freshly ground white pepper

8 cups (2 l) corn oil

For the sauce:

1 tablespoon Worcestershire sauce

3 tablespoons fine dry breadcrumbs

¼ cup (6 cl) ketchup

6 tablespoons (9 cl) oil

2 tablespoons (3 cl) wine vinegar

1 teaspoon sugar

How to prepare:

Thaw frozen fish; remove any fish bones and skin. Cut into bite-size pieces. Mix the flour with egg whites, paprika, salt, and pepper and place fish pieces into batter. Mix sauce ingredients together. Arrange the fish pieces on a platter and place the heated oil on the burner. Divide the sauce into individual bowls. Spear fish on fondue forks and fry in oil until golden brown, about 30 to 60 seconds.

Vegetarian Oil Dips

In conclusion, here are three dishes for people who do not want to eat meat or fish but still want to sit around the fondue pot and cook.

Caulifloweret Fondue

This recipe was given to us by Walter Rau, and is from his cookbook. It is especially good with cold dipping sauces.

Ingredients:

4 small heads of cauliflower

salt

fresh lemon juice

4 to 6 eggs

pinch of mace

3 tablespoons grated Parmesan cheese

1½ pounds (700 g) vegetable shortening

How to prepare:

Cut the leaves and heavy stems from cauliflower and break into flowerets. Cook in boiling salted water for 8 to 10 minutes. Drain, cool and carefully sprinkle with lemon juice (this will keep cauliflower white). While the cauliflower is cooking, beat the eggs with mace and Parmesan cheese and divide among individual bowls. Have each guest spear flowerets, cover with egg batter and fry in hot fat until crisp.

September Fondue

Ingredients:

1 pound (450 g) green beans

1 pound (450 g) mushrooms

salt

fresh lemon juice

lemon pepper

2 to 4 red bell peppers

2 cups (½ l) thick egg batter divided among 4 bowls

4 cups (1 l) oil or 2 pounds (1 kg) vegetable shortening

How to prepare:

Trim the beans and mushrooms and cut into bite-size pieces. Cook the beans for 5 minutes in boiling salted water, then drain and chill. Sprinkle the mushroom pieces with lemon juice and season with lemon pepper. Cut peppers into strips. Arrange decoratively on platter. Dip vegetables into the batter, drain, and spear a mushroom on the fork. Cook in hot fat until batter is crusty and browned and mushroom is fried.

To serve:

Serve with Aioli, Curry Sauce II, or Energy Ketchup (see recipes, pages 104 and 108).

Brussels Sprout Fondue

Ingredients:

2 pounds (1 kg) Brussels sprouts

salt

water chestnuts

1 cup (¼ l) ale or stout

6 to 8 tablespoons flour

4 eggs

pinch of freshly grated nutmeg

1½ pounds (750 g) vegetable shortening

55

How to prepare:

Trim the sprouts and cook in boiling salted water for 5 minutes. Drain and chill. Arrange decoratively on a platter with the water chestnuts. While the sprouts are cooking, beat remaining ingredients except oil to form a smooth batter. Season with salt. Let stand for 30 minutes. Divide among individual bowls. Dip Brussels sprouts and water chestnuts into batter and cook in the hot oil until browned.

To serve:

Drink the same ale with which you made the batter.

Variation:

The fried Brussels sprouts are delicious dipped into a cheese fondue.

56

Fondues for Variety Meats

Variety meats are the stepchildren when it comes to fondue cooking. But we think the time has come to mention—and applaud—some of the organ meats that are suitable for fondue. A few, such as calves and chicken livers, have already appeared in some of the recipes in this book.

Our friend Daniel Spoerri loves cooking variety meats and has a collection of at least 50 recipes for tripe, most of them from French cookbooks. We were very impressed with the Tripe in Champagne Sauce that we tasted during a visit with him in his mill near Paris. From it came the idea of combining tripe with an oil pot, and tripe with cheese fondue. The experimentation led next to cooked beef heart.

Tripe can be purchased at nearly every good butcher. It must be cooked in a pressure cooker at 15 pounds pressure for 30 to 40 minutes to make it tender enough for the fondue pot. Beef, pig, and calves hearts are cooked in salted water with juniper berries, bay leaves, and cloves until tender.

Sweetbreads have regained their importance in new German cooking. They must be blanched and pressed to retain their shape. Kidneys and liver are used raw. The pieces must be patted thoroughly dry to avoid splattering in the hot oil. It is also important not to toughen them by overcooking. Pink is better than well done; time the cooking in seconds rather than minutes. Even if you are wary of variety meats, give them a chance and try them. They are worthwhile both for taste and for low price.

Gourmet Fondue

You must try this. Your guests may start in out of politeness, but one they've tasted this fondue it will quickly disappear.

Ingredients:

2 pounds (1 kg) cooked tripe

salt

freshly ground pepper

¼ teaspoon powdered rosemary

¼ teaspoon powdered thyme

¼ teaspoon mace

4 eggs

1 teaspoon dried tarragon, crumbled

1½ cups (150 g) fine dry breadcrumbs

2 pounds (1 kg) vegetable shortening

How to prepare:

Cut tripe into bite-size squares. Grind salt, pepper, rosemary, thyme, and mace together in a mortar. Mix with tripe and refrigerate for 1 hour. Beat eggs and divide among 4 small bowls. Mix tarragon and breadcrumbs and divide among 4 plates. Place tripe squares on a platter. Heat fat and set on burner. Each guest spears tripe on a fork, dips it first in the beaten egg, then in crumb mixture, and fries it until crisp.

To serve:

This is really good with prepared remoulade sauce, and also with Apricot Chutney (see recipe, page 123).

Tripe Fondue

Here too, cooked snow-white tripe is the star attraction—this time with plenty of garlic.

Ingredients:

2 pounds (1 kg) tripe, cooked until tender

4 cloves garlic (at least)

6 eggs

1¾ cups (200 g) all-purpose flour

1 bunch Italian parsley

2 pounds (1 kg) vegetable shortening

4 ounces (120 g) bacon

1 tablespoon margarine

freshly ground pepper

How to prepare:

Cut tripe into bite-size pieces. Press the peeled cloves of garlic, mix with tripe and let stand for at least 2 hours. Beat eggs and divide among small bowls. Place flour in individual bowls. Finely chop parsley and place into a bowl. Dry the tripe and place on plate.

Heat fat. Dice bacon and fry in margarine until crisp. Season with pepper. Pour drippings into fat in fondue pot. Spear the tripe; dip first into egg, then into flour, and again into egg to coat completely. Dip into parsley and fry until golden.

Calves Heart Fondue

Ingredients:

1 calves heart or ½ beef heart

1 bunch soup greens

1 onion

10 juniper berries

2 whole cloves

salt

5 ounces (130 g) bacon

1 bunch Italian parsley

freshly ground pepper

2 pounds (1 kg) vegetable shortening

How to prepare:

Combine heart with soup greens, halved onion, juniper berries, cloves, and salt. Add water just to cover and simmer covered until heart is tender, about 1 hour. Cool, then remove all fat and tubules. Arrange individual portions of heart, bacon, and chopped parsley at each setting. Place the pepper mill on the table. Each guest sprinkles parsley and pepper to taste on the bacon slices, and wraps a small piece of bacon around each piece of heart. Spear the packet and fry in hot fat until bacon is crisp.

Kidney Mushroom Fondue

Here it is particularly important to use a fondue pot with a collar, as the kidneys and liver pieces can cause spattering when they go into the hot fat.

Ingredients:

4 to 6 not-too-large pork kidneys

fines herbes

8 ounces (225 g) small mushrooms

fresh lemon juice

freshly ground pepper

4 cups (1 l) oil or 2 pounds (1 kg) vegetable
  shortening

How to prepare:

Clean kidneys and cut crosswise into slices. Dust with fines herbes. Clean and thickly slice the mush-

57

rooms; sprinkle with lemon juice and pepper. Divide into individual portions. Spear a kidney piece between 2 mushroom slices and fry quickly in hot fat. When the mushrooms are pale brown the kidney slices will be tender.

Variation:

Kidney slices and pineapple chunks can be speared together and fried briefly—be careful; they spatter.

Sour Kidney Fondue

Ingredients:

4 cups (1 l) dry red wine

1 teaspoon pickling spice

1 teaspoon sugar

1 pound (450 g) pork or veal kidneys

1 clove garlic

2 tablespoons (3 cl) oil

salt

1 tablespoon cornstarch

1 tablespoon fresh lemon juice

How to prepare:

Tie pickling spice into a small cheesecloth bag and add to wine. Stir in sugar. Bring to boil; simmer for 10 minutes. Clean, trim, and slice the kidneys. Chop the garlic. Sauté the kidney slices and garlic quickly in hot oil in a fondue pot at the table—all the guests should help to cook and remove kidneys with their forks. Salt kidneys. Bring wine back to a boil. Remove spice bag. Mix the cornstarch and lemon juice until smooth, stir into the wine and boil until thickened. Set over a warmer. Add kidneys. Use forks to spear kidneys and also dunk bread cubes in the wine sauce.

Variations:

You can leave the wine unthickened if you wish. Halved lamb kidneys are also very good in this dish.

Sweetbread Fondue

This is best with mild mayonnaise-based sauces.

Ingredients:

1 pound (450 g) veal sweetbreads

2 cups (½ l) chicken broth

freshly grated nutmeg

1 ounce (30 g) fatty bacon

1 pound (450 g) broccoli

4 cups (1 l) oil

How to prepare:

Place the sweetbreads into boiling chicken broth, remove from range and let stand 15 to 20 minutes. Drain, cool, and remove skin carefully—they should not fall apart. Place between two boards and top with a weight until cool. Cut into slices about ½-inch thick and rub with nutmeg. Cut bacon into small pieces. Spear first a broccoli piece, then bacon and then sweetbread on fork and cook quickly—for about 1 minute—in hot oil over a burner.

Tip:

Arrange individual portions. Cut broccoli into small flowerets (not longer than 1 inch) so that it will cook quickly.

58

Berlin Lamb Liver Fondue

This must be planned in advance, as fresh lamb liver is not always easy to find.

Ingredients:

1 lamb liver (1½ to 2 pounds or 600 to 800 g)

crumbled rosemary

fines herbes

1 pound (450 g) tart apples

fresh lemon juice

lemon pepper

2 pounds (1 kg) vegetable shortening

How to prepare:

Trim all membranes and tubules from liver. Cut into bite-size, long but not too thick slices. Place in a bowl with rosemary and fines herbes and toss to coat. Let stand. Peel, quarter, and core the apples. Cut into thin slices and sprinkle with lemon juice. Pat the liver dry between paper towels. Arrange liver on platter and circle with apples. Spear an apple slice, a piece of liver, and another apple slice. Sprinkle with lemon pepper. Fry in hot oil until apple slices are lightly browned.

To serve:

Don't forget Onion Dip and Cranberry Horseradish Dip (see recipes, pages 121 and 120).

CLEAR FAVORITES

Firepots and
Boiling Broth Fondues

The newest, most stylish fondue parties in Paris, New York, and Munich are based on an old Chinese recipe—the firepot, Fondue Chinoise, or Chinese *Ho Go* or *Huo Kuo*. In these fondues the meat or fish is not fried in oil, and bread is not dunked in melted cheese; instead, lean meat and low-fat firm fish and shellfish are cooked in broth and served with low-calorie sauces. This is a fondue that weight watchers will love.

In this chapter we have assembled many recipes from all over the world—the original, variations, and a few we developed ourselves. We will tell the story of the firepot and sukiyaki in individual recipes.

You will find that these Asiatic fondues are more authentic and taste even better if they are eaten with chopsticks. We will give you directions on how to eat with chopsticks correctly, since it is easier to dunk a vegetable leaf or thin slice of meat in the broth with a chopstick or skewer than with a fork. And they won't burn your mouth.

Only wooden chopsticks or skewers should be used. Avoid plastic, silver, or ivory when cooking in hot broth. The chopsticks are used for eating; one stick stays motionless in the hand while the other is moved with the fingers. The motionless stick is held ⅔ of the way from the tapered end, positioned between the thumb and forefinger and resting against the ring finger. The square end of the chopstick is placed near the thumb, while the rounded end is held firm with the ring finger. The second chopstick is held rounded side forward between the thumb and index finger as if writing with a pencil. Both ends of the chopsticks are tapped against the table to even the points and the top stick is moved up and down against the bottom stick, the points working like pincers.

The longer you practice, the easier it will become to use chopsticks—and you may have no difficulty at all. The practice makes for a lot of fun. And Chinese and Japanese dishes really do seem to taste better eaten this way.

Basic Recipes

Our Slimming Poultry Fondue

Developed to help the chef of the cooking Klever family to lose 50 pounds and still be satisfied.

Ingredients:

For each person:

8 ounces (225 g) chicken breast and turkey slices

1 cup (100 g) thinly sliced vegetables (celery, leeks, carrots, fennel)

1 cup (¼ l) chicken broth

salt and freshly ground pepper

For 4 servings:

1 cup (¼ l) dry white wine

How to prepare:

Cut chicken and turkey into thin slices. Arrange on a platter with vegetables. Mix vegetables and broth in a pot and bring to a boil. Add wine. Place on burner and season with salt and pepper. Dip chicken and turkey speared on forks into the broth and cook until tender. At the end, pour broth with vegetables into bowls.

To serve:

On the table have salt, pepper, pickles, pickled onions and low-calorie sauces.

Note:

For one portion, there are 50 calories in the meat, 50 calories in the broth mixture, 90 calories in two slices of French bread, and 140 calories in the dips. That means 500 calories for a total meal. In comparison, 2 cups (½ l) red or white wine is 300 calories.

Chinese Fondue

Ingredients:

1 pound (450 g) beef filet or sirloin

4 cups (1 l) chicken broth

soy sauce

Sherry

4 egg yolks

How to prepare:

Cut the beef into small, paper thin rectangular slices. Season the broth with soy sauce and Sherry and let boil in the pot set over a burner. Wrap meat around the fork and cook in broth for a short time.

To serve:

Eat the meat with sauces such as mango chutney, pickled baby ears of corn, coarsely chopped celery and quartered tomatoes. After cooking, beat the hot broth into egg yolks and serve in small bowls.

Fish Fondues

Maritime Fondue

This slimming recipe without dips is 175 calories per person.

Ingredients:

8 ounces (225 g) sole fillets

fresh lemon juice

8 ounces (225 g) cooked, shelled and deveined shrimp

8 ounces (225 g) scallops

8 ounces (225 g) cleaned squid

4 cups (1 l) chicken broth

½ teaspoon dried dill weed

61

How to prepare:

Cut sole into strips and roll up. Sprinkle sole and shrimp with lemon juice. Cut scallops into thin slices, if large; slice squid. Bring chicken broth to a boil and add dill. Place over burner. Spear seafood, dip into broth and cook until tender.

Fish Fondue Theodor

Theo Ruegg received the first prize in a chefs' contest in Belgium for this recipe. He also prepares it in his Munich restaurant Chesa Ruegg.

Ingredients:

For each person:

8 ounces (225 g) sole fillets

lettuce leaves

4 cups (1 l) defatted chicken broth (can be made from bouillon cubes)

How to prepare:

Cut sole into small pieces. Arrange on a platter on top of lettuce leaves. Place a pot filled with boiling broth on the burner. Spear fish and cook in broth until white.

To serve:

Dip the cooked fish in the following special sauces. Serve with green salad and salted cooked potatoes in their jackets. The broth is served in bowls at the end.

Special Wine Sauce with Shrimp

Ingredients:

1 onion

3 tablespoons (40 g) butter

2 tablespoons flour

1 cup (¼ l) beef broth

1 cup (¼ l) white wine

2 whole cloves

4 ounces (120 g) shelled and deveined raw shrimp

pinch of salt

fresh lemon juice

How to prepare:

Dice the onions and sauté in butter until glazed. Add flour and stir briefly. Gradually stir in chicken broth and wine and cook until thickened. Add cloves and shrimp, season with salt and lemon juice and cook for 10 minutes. Serve with a ladle, for sauce to be spooned over the potatoes.

Seafood Fondue Chalet Suisse

A Swiss, Konrad Egli, devised this variation of the Chinese and Mongolian firepot and served it in his New York restaurant. Here is his recipe:

Ingredients:

1 pound (450 g) sole fillets

12 large scallops

4 lobster or langostino tails

For the fish broth:

4 cups (1 l) clam juice

2 cups (½ l) dry white wine

1 cup (¼ l) water

1 large onion

1 large carrot

1 celery stalk

62

4 white peppercorns

1 bay leaf

1/2 teaspoon salt

How to prepare:

Cut the sole fillets into 2-inch-long strips. Cut each scallop into 3 thin slices. Cut the lobster tails into bite-size pieces. Place a plate of mixed seafood in front of each guest. Combine clam juice, wine, and water in a pot and bring to a boil. Chop vegetables and add to broth along with seasonings. Simmer 30 minutes. Strain into fondue pot and place over burner. Each person cooks his own portion: Sole requires 30 to 45 seconds, scallops 1 minute and lobster 1½ minutes.

To serve:

Accompany with lemon wedges and a variety of sauces. After cooking, serve the wonderful, strong broth in individual bowls.

Tip:

Season the broth with saffron and serve with crisp toasted slices of bread which have been rubbed with garlic.

Fish Fondue Ulrich Klever

The wine for this fondue should be tart and lively—try a Mosel or white Burgundy. As always, the broth is offered for drinking at the end.

Ingredients:

1 pound (450 g) sole fillets

juice of 1 lemon

1 tablespoon soy sauce

8 ounces (225 g) carp fillets

2 tablespoons sangria

1 tablespoon Sherry

fish balls (purchased or homemade; see recipe, page 125)

8 ounces (225 g) shelled rock lobster tails

salt to taste

For the broth:

6 cups (1½ l) veal broth

1 bay leaf

5 peppercorns

salt

1 bunch fresh dill or 1 teaspoon dried

1 cup (¼ l) white wine

How to prepare:

Cut sole into slices and marinate in lemon juice and soy sauce for 1 hour. Cut carp into pieces and marinate in a mixture of sangria and Sherry. Drain fish balls (thaw if frozen) and cut lobster tails into pieces. Sprinkle with seasoned salt. Combine all broth ingredients except wine and simmer 15 minutes. Add wine and return to a boil on burner. Dip and eat as for previous recipes.

To serve:

We serve white bread with this, as well as:

Ulrich's Quick Fish Fondue Sauce

Ingredients:

1 envelope white sauce mix

1 cup (¼ l) water

1 tablespoon fresh lemon juice

3 drops Tabasco

about ½ teaspoon dried dill

63

How to prepare:

Prepare white sauce according to package directions, using water. Season with lemon juice, Tabasco, and dill. Serve hot.

Mediterranean Fondue Arne Krüger

Ingredients:

1 pound (450 g) fresh or frozen rock lobster tails or jumbo shrimp

8 ounces (225 g) high-fat melting cheese

2 onions

juice of 1 lemon

½ teaspoon instant chicken broth granules

4 cups (1 l) clear fish broth

¼ cup chopped fresh dill or 1 teaspoon dried

pinch of cayenne pepper

½ teaspoon sharp prepared mustard

½ teaspoon sugar

How to prepare:

Shell lobster and cut into bite-size pieces. Cut cheese into pieces and dice onions finely. Mix lemon juice and dehydrated broth and sprinkle over lobster. Let stand for 10 minutes. Bring the fish broth and cheese to a boil in the fondue pot and beat with a whisk until cheese is melted; keep simmering. Add onion and spices and slowly bring back to simmer. Place on burner. Spear lobster on forks and cook for about 1 minute.

To serve:

Serve with white bread and a Rhine wine.

Variety Fondue

In Japanese cooking, *Nabe* recipes are those featuring one-pot cooking at the table; each guest cooks his own food speared on skewers. You can see that *Nabe* can be translated to mean "fondue."

Ingredients:

1 pound 10 ounces (750 g) lobster meat or 12 lobster tails

1 cup (¼ l) water

2 large carrots

4 ounces (100 g) transparent noodles

8 ounces (225 g) sole fillets

4 leeks or 8 scallions

1 can Chinese mussels

4 cups (1 l) chicken broth

How to prepare:

Cut lobster into slices as thick as a finger. Bring water to a boil. Slice carrots thickly, add to water, cook until tender, and drain. Rinse with cold water. Soak noodles in cold water for 30 minutes, drain and cut into finger-length pieces. Cut the sole into bite-size pieces, dip into boiling water, drain, and rinse with cold water. Slice leeks diagonally. Drain mussels well. Arrange all ingredients attractively on one or more plates. Set the boiling broth on a burner in the middle and cook as for previous fish fondues.

Meat Fondues

Veal Skewers Bacchus

Picture on page 65

Part fish, part meat.

Veal Skewers Bacchus is a wonderful combination of meat and fish, dipped in a broth—recipe on page 64.

64

Ingredients:

For each person:

5 ounces (150 g) boneless veal loin

6 langostino or rock lobster tails

6 mushroom caps

For the broth:

chicken broth

dry white wine

thyme

rosemary

garlic

parsley

coarsely ground pepper

sage

How to prepare:

Cut veal into paper-thin slices. Spear loosely with pieces of langostino and mushrooms on wooden skewers. Prepare broth with remaining ingredients and bring to boil on a burner. Cook as for previous fondues.

To serve:

Serve with steamed rice and piquant cold and warm sauces such as Pepper Sauce, Tarragon Sauce, Tyrolean Sauce, Cumberland Sauce with Cherries and Horseradish, Curry Mayonnaise, Mango Chutney, and Pepper Pickles (see recipes).

Firepot Weishamer

Our Europeanized variation of the Oriental firepot.

Try a Mixed Meat Oriental Fondue—recipe on page 68.

Ingredients:

meat from 1/2 chicken (skinned)

1 small pork fillet

8 ounces (225 g) beef filet

4 chicken livers

8 ounces (225 g) thawed frozen shrimp (shelled and deveined)

cauliflowerets

fresh mushrooms

carrots

handful of fresh spinach leaves

1/4 cup (6 cl) Sherry

1/4 cup (6 cl) water

2 tablespoons cornstarch

4 cups (1 l) rich chicken broth

4 eggs

1/4 cup (6 cl) soy sauce

67

How to prepare:

Cut chicken into strips and pork and beef into paper-thin slices. Cube the chicken livers, blanch in boiling water and pat thoroughly dry. Cut cauliflower, mushrooms, and carrots into thin slices. Place vegetables, spinach, and meats in a pretty arrangement on the table. Beat Sherry with water and cornstarch and place in a small bowl. Let the broth boil over a burner. Before each guest place a bowl with 1 raw egg beaten with 1 tablespoon soy sauce. The host places some of the ingredients into the hot broth and cooks them for 1 to 2 minutes. Then he ladles some for each diner into a bowl with the beaten egg, to be eaten with a skewer or chopsticks. After this the guests cook their own food, not forgetting to dip each piece into the Sherry mixture. At the end, the enriched broth is divided among the bowls and sipped along with any remaining egg.

Oriental Mixed Meat Fondue

Picture on page 66

A Chinese fondue that is equally at home in Europe and the U.S.

Ingredients:

8 ounces (225 g) veal sweetbreads

2 cups (½ l) clear beef broth (can be made from bouillon cubes)

juice from ½ lemon

salt

8 ounces (225 g) veal kidneys

8 ounces (225 g) calves liver

8 ounces (225 g) veal scaloppine

6 cups (1½ l) chicken broth

1 teaspoon fines herbes

2 tablespoons (3 cl) Sherry

1 tablespoon soy sauce

How to prepare:

Blanch the sweetbreads in beef broth with lemon juice and a little salt. Drain and remove skin. Place between two boards and top with a heavy weight for several hours. Cut with a sharp knife into thin, even slices. Trim the kidneys. Cut kidneys, liver, and scaloppine into thin slices of the same thickness. Season the chicken broth with fines herbes, Sherry and soy sauce. From here on you know the rules of the game.

Tip:

Please remember that the liver and scaloppine cook in the hot broth in a few seconds; the sweetbreads and kidneys will cook in 1 to 2 minutes.

Genuine Firepots

The original Chinese or Mongolian firepot is made of brass and has a chimney in the middle (see picture, page 86). Glowing coals or alcohol are burned in the middle of the chimney. Around the charcoal holder is the bowl in which the broth boils. Today these very decorative and expensive pots can be purchased only in specialty shops.

The eating ritual is no different from that followed with a broth fondue. The Chinese always begin their firepot cooking with meat, which strengthens the broth and makes it especially good for cooking the vegetables.

Tourists in East Asia know the firepot as "Singapore Steamboat." Older Mongolian firepots may be called Dim-Lo and Shua-Yang-Jou. Lamb is always used, as Mongolians are great lamb eaters.

Mongolian Fire Pot I

Picture on page 86

Here is a recipe for a group of at least 6 persons.

Ingredients:

For 6 persons:

3 pounds (1350 g) boneless lamb leg or shoulder

4 ounces (120 g) transparent noodles

8 ounces (225 g) fresh spinach

8 stalks (225 g) celery

8 ounces (225 g) mushrooms

1 tablespoon sugar

½ cup (⅛ l) soy sauce

2 tablespoons (3 cl) peanut oil

2 tablespoons (3 cl) rice wine or pale dry Sherry

½ teaspoon Tabasco

2 tablespoons (3 cl) peanut butter

8 cups (2 l) chicken broth

68

1 leek

1 piece fresh ginger (1½ inches square)

2 cloves garlic

2 tablespoons chopped Italian parsley

How to prepare:

If frozen lamb is used, let thaw slightly; if fresh lamb, place in freezer for 2 hours. Cut lamb into paper-thin slices, then into 2-inch lengths. Arrange the slices like roof shingles on a platter. Soak transparent noodles for 30 minutes. Cut into short lengths and place on a flat plate. Wash the spinach and remove the stems. Surround the noodles with spinach leaves. Cut the celery into finger lengths and blanch in boiling water for 2 minutes. Cut the mushrooms into thin slices and place with the celery on another platter. Dissolve sugar in a little hot water. Make a sauce from the dissolved sugar, soy sauce, oil, rice wine, Tabasco, and the peanut butter dissolved in 2 tablespoons hot chicken broth and divide this among 6 bowls. Place one bowl before each guest. Mince the leek and ginger. Chop the garlic and parsley. Put the leek, ginger, garlic and parsley in the simmering broth. Dip the meat, speared on forks or skewers, in the broth and cook, then dip into sauce. At the end, add the noodles and vegetables to the broth and cook gently 1 to 2 minutes. Serve as the last course in soup bowls.

Mongolian Fire Pot II

Ingredients:

For each person:

2½ ounces (75 g) boneless lamb

2½ ounces (75 g) boneless chicken

2½ ounces (75 g) frogs' legs

2½ ounces (75 g) canned abalone

a variety of finely chopped vegetables

mushrooms

a variety of herb sauces

defatted, unsalted, rich chicken broth (see recipe, page 83)

1 egg

How to prepare:

Every guest has a Chinese soup bowl placed in front of him. At each setting there should be a fondue fork, skewers, and, if possible, a small ladle made of wire or a sieve. All the ingredients should be thinly sliced and divided among plates, platters, or bowls. Everyone cooks and eats whatever he likes, dipping the food in a variety of sauces to cool and season it. Now and then some of the broth is ladled into the bowls to drink along with the meal; for this reason, more hot broth will have to be added. At the end, each guest drops an egg into the simmering broth until it is poached soft or hard as he wishes. It is eaten with a bit more broth to conclude the meal.

69

Chrysanthemum Firepot

Picture on page 114
We ate this firepot with great satisfaction at the Hamburg restaurant Tunhuang.

Ingredients:

3 ounces (90 g) transparent noodles

oil

1 large white chrysanthemum

1 pound (450 g) celery

5 ounces (130 g) spinach leaves

8 ounces (225 g) boneless pork fillet

4 chicken breasts

4 pork kidneys

8 ounces (225 g) shrimp (shelled and deveined)

8 ounces (225 g) chicken or duck livers

12 oysters or 12 large scallops cut into thin slices

2 tablespoons (3 cl) Sherry

1 tablespoon cornstarch

2 tablespoons (3 cl) water

4 eggs

¼ cup (6 cl) soy sauce

6 cups (1½ l) clear chicken broth (can be made from bouillon cubes)

2 teaspoons salt

1 tablespoon rendered chicken fat

How to prepare:

Soak the transparent noodles in lukewarm water for 30 minutes. Drain and cut into pieces. Sauté in hot oil for 1 minute. On a platter arrange the petals of the chrysanthemum, thinly sliced celery, the sautéed noodles, the washed and dried spinach leaves, the pork, chicken, and kidneys, sliced paper-thin, halved shrimp, sliced liver, and the shelled oysters. Mix the Sherry, cornstarch, and water and sprinkle over the various meats. Before each guest place a bowl in which 1 egg has been beaten with 1 table-spoon soy sauce. Salt the boiling broth and add the chicken fat. Place portion sizes of vegetables, noo-dles, meat and shrimp in the pot and cook 2 to 3 minutes; remove. The hostess then adds the chrysanthemum petals to the bouillon.

Note:

Adding the flower petals is a decorative flourish; in our own Chinese cookbook the Chrysanthemum Firepot does not include chrysanthemum petals.

Variations:

Preparation and cooking remain the same, but change ingredients as follows:
1 chrysanthemum

1 pound (450 g) leeks cut into thick rings

4 ounces (120 g) transparent noodles

bamboo shoots from an 8-ounce (225 g) can

10 ounces (300 g) pork fillet

8 ounces (225 g) beef sirloin

2 pieces Belgian endive in thick rings

6 large scallops cut into thin slices

8 ounces (225 g) shrimp

12 stuffed grape leaves

Ten-in-One Pot

An adaptation and simplification of Shih-Chin-Nuan-Kuo from the Time-Life book *The Cooking of China.*

Ingredients:

For 6 persons:

8 dried Chinese mushrooms (not the black tree ears or cloud ears)

2 ounces (60 g) transparent noodles

8 ounces (225 g) Chinese cabbage

1 pound (450 g) spinach leaves

12 slices bamboo shoots (¼ inch thick)

2 slices cooked ham

12 fish balls (from a jar or homemade—see recipe, page 125)

12 thin slices beef (cut into small oblong pieces)

2 tablespoons butter

ground star anise

5 tablespoons (8 cl) soy sauce

2 teaspoons rice wine

70

12 small slices pork leg

1½ teaspoons sugar

salt

1 clove garlic

4 eggs

8 ounces (225 g) ground pork

2 teaspoons cornstarch

6 cups (1½ l) chicken broth

1 tablespoon sesame oil

additional soy sauce for dipping

How to prepare:

Soak mushrooms in lukewarm water for 30 minutes. Trim stems and discard. Halve the mushroom caps. Soak the noodles in lukewarm water for 30 minutes, drain, and cut into pieces. Cut the Chinese cabbage into strips. Blanch in boiling water for 1 minute, then drain well. Tear the spinach leaves into small pieces. Arrange all these ingredients on a platter with the bamboo shoots, ham (cut into strips), and the drained fish balls. Sauté the beef slices in butter until they lose their red color, then season with star anise, 2 tablespoons of the soy sauce, and rice wine and continue sautéing. Rub the pork slices with ½ teaspoon of the sugar, some salt, 1 tablespoon soy sauce, and the finely chopped garlic and broil until crisp. Beat eggs and make 6 thin omelets. Mix the ground pork with the remaining soy sauce, cornstarch, sugar, and a little salt. Use to fill omelets; roll up to enclose pork. Arrange on a steamer above boiling water and steam, covered, for 15 minutes. Cut into slices. Arrange all dipping ingredients on platters. Bring the chicken broth to a boil in a saucepan. Place the Chinese cabbage, spinach, and noodles into the firepot. Lay ham, fish balls, mushrooms, beef, filled egg pancakes, pork, and bamboo shoots on top. Over these 10 foods, carefully pour hot broth; avoid disturbing and mixing foods. Simmer for 10 minutes. Every guest should have a small bowl with a dipping sauce of soy sauce and sesame oil. Each person serves himself with a fork or skewer.

Boiled Meat Fondue

Picture on page 76

Ingredients:

6 cups (1½ l) clear beef broth

2 pounds (1 kg) boneless beef chuck or shoulder

1 leek

2 carrots

1 parsnip

4 peppercorns

½ bay leaf

How to prepare:

Bring the broth to a boil. Cut the meat into 2-inch-long and 1-inch-wide pieces, add to broth, and cook for 1 hour or until tender. Clean and thinly slice leek, carrots, and parsnip. Add the vegetables, peppercorns, and bay leaf to the broth and cook another 30 minutes. (Alternatively, everything can be cooked in a pressure cooker under pressure for 30 minutes.) Place the fondue pot on a burner, pour in the broth and boiled meat pieces, and bring to a boil. Spear out the meat with a fondue fork.

To serve:

Team with farmer's bread, coarse salt, cornichons, horseradish with and without cream, cranberries, Cranberry Horseradish Dip (see recipe, page 120), and mustard.

Russian Fondue

Based on the Boiled Meat Fondue, this is a soup fondue made with a strong broth and filled dumplings called Pelmeny, that were customarily served to the coachmen in Russia. The dumplings can be prepared long before the party and frozen, as they once were in the ice houses of Russia. This fondue is good for a large group.

71

Ingredients:

For the dough:

about 8 cups (1 kg) all-purpose flour

6 eggs

For the first filling:

1 onion

10 ounces (300 g) ground beef

3 ounces (90 g) ground pork

salt

freshly ground pepper

garlic powder

½ cup (⅛ l) water

For the second filling:

8 ounces (225 g) red snapper fillets, ground

4 ounces (120 g) finely chopped shrimp

salt

dill

handful of finely chopped spinach

For the third filling:

8 ounces (225 g) sauerkraut

2 ounces (60 g) bacon

8 ounces (225 g) ground smoked pork

salt

freshly ground pepper

caraway seed

10 cups (2½ l) clear beef broth

wine vinegar

How to prepare:

Mix and knead a noodle dough of flour, eggs and enough water to make a dough that can be rolled very thin. Roll out dough and cut rounds 2½ inches in diameter with a glass or cookie cutter. For the first filling, finely chop onion and mix with the remaining ingredients, seasoning well (the water will help filling stay juicy). Mix the ground fish with the shrimp, seasonings and spinach for the second filling. For the third filling, press sauerkraut dry and chop finely. Cut bacon into small cubes and fry until crisp. Mix sauerkraut, bacon, and smoked pork and season heavily.

Place 1 teaspoon filling on each round of dough, brush edges with water and fold over, pressing edges to seal. Pinch the ends of the turnover together so each pelmeny resembles a little hat. Arrange them on a cloth-covered board or on cookie sheets and place in freezer until hard (this will keep them from sticking together). Remove from cookie sheets and store in plastic bags or foil in freezer.

When the guests have arrived, place the first batch of frozen pelmeny into the hot broth placed over a burner. Stir to keep dough pockets from sticking on the bottom or bursting. Cook gently for 15 minutes; they are done when they float.

To serve:

Each guest gets a saucer in which he puts a little wine vinegar for seasoning the pelmeny. Either host or guest retrieves the pelmeny from the broth (or the host divides them), adds a little broth to them and enjoys; then the second batch goes into more broth, which should be kept boiling in the kitchen. The 15 minutes it takes to cook the next pelmeny provide a good excuse to pause for a cold vodka or beer.

Tip:

If any of the fillings is not thick enough, add some dry breadcrumbs; but be careful not to overdo the crumbs or the filling will be dry.

72

Hard-to-Please Fondues

You can make a broth fondue with any number of different ingredients. The soup base can be beef, veal, or chicken (see recipes, page 83). Here are suggestions for a variety of novel additions:

White Bread Cubes:

Brown bread cubes on all sides in butter. Beat 1 egg with 6 tablespoons (9 cl) milk, pinch of salt and freshly grated nutmeg. Pour this over the cubes and toss to coat. Fry in butter until golden brown.

Bread with Marrow:

Toast thin slices of French bread. Arrange slices of marrow on a slotted spoon and hold in hot bouillon for a short time (you can do this at the table if you wish). Drain and serve on toast, seasoning with salt and pepper. Eat with broth or float it on top.

Steamed Egg Custard:

Beat together 2 eggs, ¼ cup (6 cl) milk, pinch of salt, freshly ground pepper and freshly grated nutmeg. Pour into a buttered pan or casserole and steam above boiling water for 30 minutes. Unmold. Cut into slices or cubes.

Variation 1:

Mix with a generous amount of finely chopped parsley, chervil, or dill.

Variation 2:

Add 1 tablespoon tomato paste and pinch of sugar to eggs.

Variation 3:

Mix in 1 teaspoon sweet paprika.

Farina Dumplings:

Mix 1 egg, 1 teaspoon melted butter, 3 tablespoons farina, salt, freshly grated nutmeg, and a small pinch baking powder. Let stand for 10 minutes. Scoop out small dumplings with a wet spoon and drop into the bubbling broth. When dumplings float, cover and simmer 15 minutes. This will make about 8 dumplings; it can be multiplied to make as many as you like. You can also use packaged dumpling mix.

Tip:

The dumplings taste even better sprinkled with chopped chives.

Liver Spaetzle:

Mix 4 ounces (120 g) ground beef or pork liver with ½ onion finely chopped, chopped parsley, about 6 heaping tablespoons dry breadcrumbs, 1 egg, 2 tablespoons melted butter, salt and a pinch of marjoram. Press through a colander into the simmering broth. Simmer 5 minutes, remove with a slotted spoon and serve.

Quick Dumplings:

Sauté 1 tablespoon finely chopped parsley in 2 tablespoons butter. Beat 1 egg with salt, pepper and sweet paprika. Stir in 2 tablespoons dry breadcrumbs and butter/parsley mixture. Shape with the hands into small balls, add to the simmering soup and let simmer 10 minutes. Remove and serve.

Variations:

Mix in finely chopped mushrooms, ham, shrimp, or chicken.

We could also write about the recipes for the Japanese poultry and vegetable fondue *Tori Mizutaki*, or *Shabu Shabu* (beef and vegetables in chicken broth), but these are essentially repetitions of the firepot: One cooks finely chopped meat and different vegetables in hot broth. Simply invent your own special firepot fondues and give them an exotic-sounding name!

More Ideas

Italian Tomato Fondue

That's what we call this variation in which foods are cooked in a red meat soup.

Ingredients:

1 pound (450 g) skinned and boned chicken breasts

1 pound (450 g) veal leg

73

2 pounds (1 kg) small, tart tomatoes

2 onions

¼ cup (6 cl) olive oil

1 tablespoon sugar

1 teaspoon salt

1 teaspoon dried oregano

freshly ground pepper

2 tablespoons (3 cl) tomato paste

about 5 cups (1¼ l) chicken broth

4 ounces (120 g) grated Parmesan cheese

How to prepare:

Freeze the raw meat for about 2 hours. Slice the tomatoes, dice the onions and sauté both in oil (the onions should remain firm). Add sugar, salt, oregano, pepper, and tomato paste and simmer 20 minutes. Press the tomato mixture through a sieve to puree and stir in 4 cups (1 l) chicken broth. Place over the burner. Cut the frozen meat into paper-thin slices and cook in the tomato broth. Each guest dips the meat into Parmesan cheese set in a small bowl at his place.

Variations:

Season the broth with garlic or stir in 2 to 3 tablespoons Italian salad dressing at the table.

Punsch Fondue

Here is a fondue that does not use either fat or broth.

Ingredients;

6 cups (1½ l) red wine (Beaujolais is good)

5 pink peppercorns

10 black peppercorns

1 whole clove

10 coriander seeds

½ cinnamon stick

1 bay leaf

1 tablespoon sugar

2 teaspoons salt

1 teaspoon coarsely ground pepper

1 teaspoon garlic salt

1¾ pounds (800 g) beef filet or sirloin

How to prepare:

Place wine in fondue pot. Tie pink peppercorns, black peppercorns, clove, coriander, cinnamon stick, and bay leaf in a cheesecloth bag and add to the wine. Bring to a boil. Add sugar. Combine salt and coarsely ground pepper in a dry cast-iron skillet and toast, crushing them with a wooden spoon. Add garlic salt and divide this mixture among small plates. Cut the meat into thin, small slices and cook in wine, then dip into seasoned salt.

To serve:

Have warm Garlic Bread (see recipe, page 126) or French Bread (page 129) on the table.

Variations:

This fondue can also be made with white wine. Instead of beef, use chicken or veal.

Sukiyaki

Now to the fondue that represents Japanese cooking. Called "ski-ya-ki"—the "u" is silent—Sukiyaki is *the* typical Japanese recipe. The name, though, is misleading; the word *sukiyaki* refers to hunters' and shepherds' practice of broiling meat "on a plowshare," but the dish as we know it consists of meat and vegetables cooked in a spiced liquid. Recipe variations are numerous, but the preparation is always the same. With sukiyaki one always drinks beer.

Author's style of Sukiyaki, served in the original pot—recipe on page 77.

Sukiyaki, My Style

Picture page 75
We brought this first recipe back from Japan and adapted it to suit Western tastes.

Ingredients:

1½ to 2 pounds (650 to 900 g) rump steak

8 ounces (225 g) onions

8 ounces (225 g) carrots

8 ounces (225 g) leeks

4 ounces (120 g) Boston lettuce

1 small can bamboo shoots

1 small can bean sprouts (fresh are even better)

6 Chinese mushrooms

handful of spinach leaves

4 ounces (120 g) tofu (soybean curd)

2 cups (½ l) chicken broth

1 tablespoon soy sauce

1 tablespoon mirin (sweet rice wine) or pale dry Sherry

1 teaspoon fines herbes

pinch of sugar

2 tablespoons (3 cl) oil

4 to 8 egg yolks

2 to 3 cups (200 to 300 g) cooked rice

How to prepare:

Cut the meat into paper-thin slices the size of a playing card. Arrange decoratively on white or black platters. Cut onions into paper-thin slices, carrots into thin julienne pieces, and leeks into diagonal slices. Cut the lettuce into strips and the bamboo shoots into thin slices or rounds. Drain the bean sprouts and pull them apart. Soak the mushrooms in lukewarm water until soft, cut away the hard stems and slice the caps into strips. Cut the spinach leaves into squares with kitchen shears. Slice bean curd thinly. Arrange everything on platters attractively. Mix the chicken broth with the soy sauce and wine and season with fines herbes and sugar (the soy sauce will serve for the necessary salt). Heat the liquid in a saucepan. In the sukiyaki pot—the genuine article is made of iron and looks like a strong springform pan—brown some of the meat slices and some of the vegetables in a little oil. Fill with broth to the depth of two fingers and cook over the burner. Provide each guest with a bowl containing a raw egg yolk and a bowl of cooked rice. The host divides the food in the pot and each diner eats out of his own bowl, in which the egg is mixed with the vegetables and meat. (Have a second egg yolk ready for each guest.) There should only be enough broth in the pot to braise the food, not to boil it. After the first round, have each person cook his own food as for a European fondue. Sukiyaki is only eaten with chopsticks, and traditionally the diners kneel at a low table.

77

Everyday Sukiyaki

Ingredients:

1 pound (450 g) beef filet or sirloin

1 pound (450 g) leeks

8 ounces (225 g) spinach or Boston lettuce

5 ounces (150 g) fresh mushrooms or ¼ cup (20 g) dried shiitake mushrooms

1 small can bamboo shoots

2 ounces (60 g) rice noodles (shirataki)

a few pieces beef kidney fat

1 tablespoon soy sauce

1 teaspoon sugar

1 teaspoon sake (rice wine)

4 eggs

unsalted dry cooked rice

Fondue fans who want to try something new should try the hearty Boiled Meat Fondue—recipe on page 71.

How to prepare:

Cut the beef into thin slices. Cut the leeks into 2-inch slices, the spinach or lettuce leaves into strips, the mushrooms (dried mushrooms should be soaked first) and the bamboo shoots into julienne strips. Drop the rice noodles into boiling water. As soon as it returns to a boil, drain and cut noodles into finger-length pieces.

Place the sukiyaki pot on a burner and heat. Rub pot with pieces of kidney fat and allow fat to melt. Add the soy sauce, sugar, and sake. When all is hot, add some of the vegetables. Stew for 10 minutes; the vegetables will add flavor to the liquid. Add some of the meat slices; cook until brown.

Add the rice noodles to the pot. Place a bowl with a beaten raw egg and a bowl of rice before each guest. Continue to add ingredients to pot while eating. It may be necessary to add more kidney fat, soy sauce, and sake.

Japanese Sukiyaki

The meat for this dish should be well marbled with fat. Particularly suitable is prime rib, the best and most expensive of which comes from Kobe beef. The Kobe bulls are massaged daily with alcohol so that the fat is well distributed in the muscles and the meat looks like a piece of marble. They are also given beer to drink in the last year before they are slaughtered.

Ingredients:

1 pound (450 g) boneless beef

1 can bamboo shoots

6 scallions

1 large onion

6 mushrooms

12 tofu cubes (soybean curd)

8 ounces (225 g) rice noodles

bunch of watercress

piece of beef kidney fat

6 tablespoons (9 cl) soy sauce

3 to 4 tablespoons sugar

6 tablespoons (9 cl) rice wine (sake)

How to prepare:

Cut the meat, vegetables, and tofu into thin slices. Put the rice noodles into boiling water; when water returns to boil, drain and cut noodles into small pieces. Arrange everything, including the watercress and rice noodles, attractively on a platter. Heat the sukiyaki pan and rub with the kidney fat. Add the first 6 slices of beef. Pour soy sauce over and sprinkle with sugar. Turn the meat after 1 minute and coat with liquid. Push the meat to one side, add about ⅓ of the other ingredients to the pan, and pour sake over. Simmer for 5 minutes, adding a little water if necessary, and it is ready to eat. This sukiyaki variation is not served with egg.

Beef Fondue Puegogi

This fondue from Korea uses a sukiyaki pot that is very like a European fondue pot. Use Chinese porcelain spoons or regular tablespoons and small plates.

Broth:

3 cups (¾ l) very strong chicken broth

2 cups (½ l) soy sauce

scant 2 ounces (50 g) ginseng root

4 ounces (120 g) canned bamboo shoots

4 ounces (120 g) bean sprouts (fresh or canned)

scant 2 ounces (50 g) fresh ginger

1 green bell pepper

4 ounces (120 g) fresh mushrooms

4 ounces (120 g) carrots

5 cloves garlic

salt

freshly ground pepper

1 sprig fresh or ¼ teaspoon dried mint

For each person you will need:

4 thin, warm Rice Flour Pancakes about 4 inches in diameter (see recipe, page 126)

4 ounces (120 g) ¼-inch-thick, 1½-inch-wide beef filet slices

1 ounce (30 g) thinly sliced calves liver

2 ounces (60 g) finely chopped chicken breast with skin

1 ounce (30 g) canned shrimp (drain and reserve liquid)

regular soy sauce and kecap manis (sweet soy sauce) for dipping

How to prepare:

Mix the chicken broth and soy sauce in the sukiyaki pot. Clean all vegetables listed through the carrots and cut into fine julienne strips. Add garlic and spices to the cold chicken broth mixture, place on burner, and cook for 10 minutes.

To serve:

In front of each guest have his portion of meat and shrimp attractively arranged. The rice flour pancakes should be stacked on another plate. On the table are two bowls, one with regular and one with sweet soy sauce, each mixed with some of the juice drained from the canned shrimp.

Each person places a sampling of the foods on a spoon and stands it (if using a porcelain spoon) or holds it (if using a tablespoon) in the broth until it is tender and cooked to taste. Take a rice flour pancake and place the cooked food on it, adding some of the mushrooms and vegetables from the broth, then roll up the pancake. The filled rice cake is eaten out of hand, and before every bite is dipped into both soy sauces.

Other Firepots from the Orient

Vietnamese Firepot

We have given in this and the following recipe the original ingredients as well as other possible ingredients, just in case some are hard to find. All the original ingredients can be purchased in East Asian markets.

Ingredients:

8 ounces (225 g) boneless beef sirloin

5 ounces (150 g) boned and skinned chicken breast

4 ounces (120 g) fish fillets

5 ounces (150 g) cleaned fresh squid

5 ounces (150 g) cooked, shelled, and deveined shrimp

8 ounces (225 g) fresh bean sprouts

bunch of fresh coriander

1 scallion

bunch of fresh mint

1 head Boston lettuce

1 cucumber

2 lemons

1 jar pickled pearl onions

10 Rice Pancakes (see recipe, page 126)

milk from 2 coconuts or ½ cup (⅛ l) water and 1 cup (¼ l) lukewarm milk

8 ounces (225 g) transparent noodles

1 onion

1 jar sweet and sour sauce

79

1 can Hoisin sauce or Oriental chili sauce

¼ cup (6 cl) Nuoc-mam sauce (thinned) or ½ cup (⅛ l) bottled sukiyaki sauce

¼ cup (6 cl) Nuoc-mam sauce

pinch of sugar

freshly ground pepper

salt

2 tablespoons (3 cl) oil

1 clove garlic

How to prepare:

Have the butcher cut the beef into paper-thin slices. Pat the chicken breasts dry with paper towels and slice diagonally. Rinse the fish and squid, pat dry and cut into bite-size pieces. Halve the shrimp lengthwise. Rinse the sprouts and drain. Chop the coriander and scallion finely; leave the mint sprigs whole. Clean the lettuce, wash and dry well. Scrub the cucumber under hot water, then slice thinly with a slicer or mandoline. Scrub the lemons under hot water, dry and cut into thin slices. Drain the pearl onions. Quarter the rice pancakes and soak in the coconut milk or the water/milk mixture to soften, then arrange in a single layer on a damp towel. Cook the noodles in boiling water for 5 minutes, then drain through a sieve. Slice the onion into thin rings.

All the prepared ingredients, except for the transparent noodles and rice pancakes, should be arranged on a large serving platter or a lazy susan. Place the sweet and sour sauce, Hoisin sauce, and thinned Nuoc-mam sauce in bowls in the middle, then arrange the beef, chicken breast, fish fillets, squid and shrimp around them like a rosette. Around the outer edge of the plate should be the cucumber slices, pearl onions, bean sprouts and lettuce leaves, garnished with mint sprigs and lemon slices. Layer the rice pancakes on a plate while the broth comes to a boil.

For the broth, combine the coconut milk or the water/milk mixture in a saucepan with the transparent noodles, Nuoc-mam sauce, sugar, pepper, and salt. Add the oil and pressed garlic. Cook briefly, and then transfer to a firepot or sukiyaki pot. Place the

boiling broth over the lowest flame of a burner or over a candle warmer placed in the center of the table.

To serve:

Each serves himself, holding the food in the broth with a skewer or fondue fork. Place some raw or cooked vegetables on the quartered rice pancake, top with the cooked meat or fish, roll up and dip in the sauces. The pancake rolls should be eaten with the fingers.

Hints:

The foods should not be cooked too long. This tastes especially good if some of the ingredients are left raw.

Vietnamese Vinegar Pot

A recipe we love from Tien Huu's book, *The Magic of Vietnamese Cooking*. For this we use a large wooden lazy susan, along with bowls or small plates and skewers or fondue forks.

Ingredients:

1 pound 5 ounces (600 g) boneless lean beef

½ teaspoon freshly ground pepper

½ teaspoon salt

1 large coconut

2 cups (½ l) wine vinegar

1 teaspoon oil

2 tablespoons (3 cl) Nuocmam sauce

2 teaspoons sugar

1 clove garlic

1 fresh pineapple

1 head Boston lettuce

8 ounces (225 g) fresh bean sprouts

1 jar (12 ounces or 350 g) pickled pearl onions

80

1 cucumber

bunch of mint

bunch of fresh coriander

2 onions

10 Rice Pancakes (see recipe, page 126)

1 small bottle kecap manis (sweet soy sauce)

juice of 2 lemons

How to prepare:

Pat meat dry on paper towels and cut across the grain into thin slices, then cut into 2-inch strips. Salt and pepper lightly. Pierce a hole in 2 of the eyes of the coconut and drain out the milk. Mix half of the milk with the vinegar, the oil, the Nuoc-mam sauce, 1 teaspoon of the sugar, and the pressed garlic. Bring to a boil, then pour into the firepot.

Cut off the pineapple skin, slice the fruit, then dice the slices, cutting away the hard middle core. Separate lettuce into leaves, wash leaves and drain whole. Rinse bean sprouts with boiling water and drain. Drain the pickled onions. Scrub the cucumber under hot water and cut (with the skin) into very thin slices. Leave the mint and coriander sprigs whole. Slice the onions into thin rings. Quarter the rice pancakes, dip into coconut milk and arrange in single layer on damp towels.

For the sauce, mix half of the kecap manis with the remaining 1 teaspoon sugar, the lemon juice and 3 tablespoons of finely chopped pineapple. Leave the rest of the kecap manis plain. Place the sauce bowls in the center of a lazy susan or large serving platter. Arrange all the ingredients neatly and decoratively on the platter—beef, lettuce, sprouts, pearl onions, and cucumber slices. Garnish with mint and coriander sprigs. Place the firepot over a burner set on low flame or over a candle warmer. Place the platter or lazy susan next to it. The rice pancakes are layered on a plate.

To serve:

Everyone takes skewers or fondue forks and cooks meat in the broth. In between, prepare a rice pancake and/or lettuce leaf in a bowl or on a plate, add-ing accompaniments as desired and flavoring with a few leaves stripped from the mint and coriander. Using a skewer or fork, remove the meat from the broth, place it on the lettuce or pancake and roll up into a packet. Dip it into sauce before each bite.

Hints:

Instead of using the drained coconut milk, you can puree half of the coconut meat in the food processor, add hot water to cover, let stand 10 minutes, then press out all liquid. A mixture of half water and half milk can also be substituted. Rice pancakes are dried, transparent, round cakes, about 10 inches in diameter, made of rice flour. They are found in Oriental markets or make them according to the recipe on page 126.

Fish Fondue Katou

81

Ingredients:

1 pound (450 g) halibut

8 ounces (225 g) boneless shark

8 ounces (225 g) boneless trout

juice of 2 lemons

salt

freshly ground white pepper

12 large scallops (fresh or frozen)

4 cups (1 l) meat or chicken broth

curry powder or saffron

How to prepare:

Cut the fish into bite-size pieces, mix with lemon juice and marinate for 1 hour. Drain and dry fish. Sprinkle the shark with pepper. Dip scallops into boiling water to blanch; drain. Heat the broth, place over the burner and season with curry or saffron to taste (saffron should be soaked in a little water, then added). When broth boils, begin cooking.

Chinese Scampi

Ingredients:

1 pound (450 g) jumbo shrimp or North Sea langostino tails

a few lettuce leaves

1 can squid

1 can mussels

3 cups (¾ l) clear beef broth

fresh dill

½ cup (100 g) butter

salt

Tabasco

How to prepare:

Arrange the shrimp on lettuce leaves. Drain the squid and mussels, dry well and add to shrimp. Bring broth to a boil. Finely chop dill and mash with the butter, a little salt and Tabasco. Divide mixture among 4 individual bowls. Let broth boil on top of the burner. Spear a shrimp, squid and a mussel alternately on skewer and simmer 1 minute. Dip while hot into the dill butter, then into the sauces.

To serve:

Dip into Aioli and Hazelnut Sauce (see recipes, pages 104 and 109). Rice can also be served.

Nouvelle Cuisine Fondue

The Japanese have always eaten their fish raw; it tastes marvelous if the fish is really fresh and is cut into paper-thin slices. Nouvelle cuisine also offers raw salmon and raw scallops as an appetizer—Le Duc, on the Boulevard Raspail in Paris, specializes in raw fish. Here is a fondue for when you want something different.

Ingredients:

8 ounces (225 g) large scallops

8 ounces (225 g) raw boneless tuna

8 ounces (225 g) raw boneless salmon

8 ounces (225 g) flounder fillets

8 ounces (225 g) halibut fillets

fresh lemon juice

best-quality olive oil

best-quality walnut oil

crème fraîche or sour cream

green peppercorns

How to prepare:

We figure on 8 ounces (225 g) of really fresh fish for each person; those mentioned above are just suggestions, but you must use saltwater, not freshwater, species. Place in freezer for a short time until firm, then slice paper-thin with a sharp knife or electric knife. Arrange on one or two platters. Place lemon juice, olive oil, and walnut oil in small separate pitchers. Have bowls of crème fraîche and green peppercorns on the table.

To serve:

Take a piece of raw fish and season to your taste. Cooked potatoes in their jackets can also be served. Dry Champagne makes the perfect drink. In order to maintain the "dip" character—this is, after all, a fondue book—place two bowls with the following dipping marinades on the table:

Two Marinades for Raw Fish

Mix:

2 tablespoons (3 cl) Sherry vinegar with 3 tablespoons (5 cl) nut oil, chopped chervil, and salt and pepper.

Mix:

1 tablespoon finely chopped chives with 3 tablespoons (5 cl) plain yogurt, 3 tablespoons (5 cl) crème

fraîche and 1 tablespoon fresh lime or lemon juice. Season with a few chopped green peppercorns.

Sweet and Sour Pork Fondue

One last recipe to serve as a transition—before we move on to other, not-quite-fondue dishes that are cooked at the table.

Ingredients:

1¾ pounds (800 g) roast pork shoulder

1 hot red pepper

3 tablespoons cornstarch

1 cup (¼ l) wine vinegar

1 cup (200 g) firmly packed brown sugar

2 green bell peppers

2 tablespoons (3 cl) sauce picante

1 tablespoon sharp prepared mustard

1 tablespoon Worcestershire sauce

1 can pineapple chunks

How to prepare:

Cut the cooled roasted pork into finger-thick strips. Seed the pepper and chop finely. Mix the cornstarch with the vinegar and cook with the sugar in a fondue pot until thickened and clear. Core, seed, and dice the peppers. Add the spices, peppers, and pineapple with juice to the pot. Cover and simmer 10 minutes, then place on the burner. Spear pork on fondue forks and heat in pot.

To serve:

Accompany with bowls of cooked rice. A spoonful of the broth (with peppers and pineapple) can be poured over each serving of rice.

Chicken and Fish Broths for Fondue

Clear Chicken Broth

Ingredients:

bones from 2 chickens or a stewing chicken

3 large onions

1 carrot

1 piece celery root

1 bouquet garni (parsley, celery leaves, fresh dill, etc., as you wish)

egg white

fresh lemon juice

dry white wine

salt to taste

How to prepare:

Combine the bones, chopped into small pieces, the unpeeled whole onions, the scraped carrot and celery root, and bouquet garni in a pot and cover with water. Cover and simmer for 4 hours. Strain broth, chill and remove fat. Measure the broth, warm, and for every 4 cups (1 liter) beat in 1 egg white, 1 teaspoon lemon juice, and 2 tablespoons (3 cl) white wine. Bring to a boil and skim off foam. Strain through several thicknesses of cheesecloth. Season lightly with salt; this broth is so strong that a very little will suffice.

Fish Broth

A good basic recipe for fish broth is the one used in Seafood Fondue Chalet Suisse (see recipe, page 62). Alternatively, cover 2 pounds (1 kg) fish bones and heads with plenty of water, add seasonings and several unpeeled onions as desired, and simmer gently 2 to 3 hours. Strain broth and add dry wine to taste.

83

BY ANY OTHER NAME

Fondues in Their Broadest Sense

In this book, what we have so far understood as fondue is any food that is cooked at the table and eaten from one pot. Now we want to stretch this friendly, democratic culinary concept to include other dishes that are prepared at the table. Some are favorite traditional recipes; others were developed expressly for this volume. In a few of these recipes we use table stoves of different types. These are made in many models, the greatest difference among them being whether you cook in one large pan or whether each person in the group has his own.

You will see in reading these recipes that you often come back to the conventional fondue equipment. An enthusiast will want to acquire the special equipment—chiefly because, when you have found that a recipe suits you, you can then make it frequently and with no trouble.

We have included a few recipes using the Japanese cast-iron grill called a hibachi, as well as other grills. If you enjoy a sociable fondue, you will surely want to try other dishes involving tabletop grilling. Even if you're skeptical as to whether these recipes really belong in a fondue book, we urge you to try them.

Wine Fondue

Ingredients:

2 cups (1/2 l) white wine

2 ounces (60 g) grated almonds

2 tarragon leaves

1 cup (1/4 l) defatted veal or chicken broth

pinch of salt

2 thin slices fresh ginger or 1 teaspoon ground

For dipping:

the diced meat from 1 cooked stewing chicken, skinned, or cubes of skinned veal breast meat

toasted white bread cubes

Bagna Cauda is an authentic recipe from Italy's Piedmont—recipe on page 88.

How to prepare:

Combine the wine, almonds, and tarragon in the pot and heat over a small flame; do not boil. Fill with broth. Stir in salt and ginger and set on burner.

To serve:

Dip the meat in the simmering broth until heated through, or soak the bread cubes. Dips are not necessary, but freshly ground pepper, mustard fruits, and cranberries are good accompaniments. Serve with plates and forks as for other meat fondues.

Tip:

You can also dip paper-thin-sliced steak or raw veal in the simmering broth.

Westphalian Sausage Fondue

This time a thicker, brandy-flavored broth is used for dunking.

Ingredients:

1 pound (450 g) beef chuck or shin

2 soup bones

bunch of soup greens

2 onions

1 chicken bouillon cube

2 ounces (60 g) pearl barley

salt

freshly ground pepper

allspice

3 tablespoons (4 cl) German brandy

freshly grated nutmeg

How to prepare:

Cover beef and bones with water in pressure cooker, bring to a boil uncovered and skim foam several times. Simmer 30 minutes; remove bones. Add the washed soup greens, the unpeeled onions and the bouillon cube and cook under pressure for 50 minutes. Meanwhile, cook the pearl barley in water until tender. Strain the broth. Cut the meat into small cubes and grind it with the drained barley. Stir in enough broth to make a thick, creamy mixture. Place in pot on top of burner and season well with salt, pepper, and allspice. Stir in brandy and sprinkle with nutmeg.

To serve:

Dip with dark bread or Snacks (see recipe, page 128).

Fondue Ranchero

The preparation is easy enough for a child; the hard part is finding really good potatoes for dunking. Best suited are small new potatoes, which must be halved if large. They are cooked and speared with their skins, and cut in one or two places so they will hold as much of the corned beef mixture as possible. Other firm potatoes can be used cooked, unpeeled and quartered.

Ingredients:

1 pound (450 g) corned beef slices

1 can (12 ounces or 340 g) corned beef

1 cup (¼ l) beef broth (can be made with bouillon cube)

1 tablespoon cornstarch

2 tablespoons (3 cl) water

3 tablespoons (4 cl) tequila or gin

How to prepare:

Heat the corned beef slices in the fondue pot. Dice the canned corned beef and add along with broth. Stir until diced meat melts. Mix the cornstarch and water until smooth and stir into broth to thicken. Cook briefly. Add tequila or gin at the table after pot has been set over burner.

To serve:

Fondue Ranchero is dipped up with potatoes or bread. Banana chunks are also very good for dunking.

87

It is said that the Mongolian Firepot is the oldest fondue—recipe on page 68.

Bagna Cauda

A famous traditional fondue from Italy's Piedmont region. Raw seasonal vegetables are dipped in a garlicky sauce which is kept warm in a fondue pot on the table; originally, a small ceramic pot was placed in front of each person.

The Italians, who use fennel, cucumber, scallions, and quartered small tomatoes, place the vegetables for a short time in ice water. This leaches out some of the vitamins, but makes the vegetables crisp and cools the sauce so that the mouth is not burned so easily. Instead of bread there are thin breadsticks, called *grissini*, that are available in large supermarkets and Italian groceries.

Bagna Cauda I

Picture on page 85
Here is our personal recipe. The name of the dish, which means "warm bath," is pronounced "Banya cowda." We like to drink rosé with this.

Ingredients:

½ cup (⅛ l) olive oil

8 ounces (225 g) anchovy fillets

6 garlic cloves

6 tablespoons (9 cl) heavy cream

vegetables of the season, some raw, some blanched, for example

8 ounces (225 g) cauliflowerets

8 ounces (225 g) broccoli

1 pound (450 g) celery

1 green and 1 red bell pepper

8 ounces (225 g) carrots

8 ounces (225 g) mushrooms

1 can artichoke hearts

How to prepare:

Heat the oil in a pan. Add the drained and mashed anchovies and mashed garlic and cook gently, stirring and mashing the anchovies and garlic further. As the mixture becomes homogenized, stir in the cream; when it has become a thick sauce, pour it into the fondue pot or into individual bowls. Keep warm over the smallest flame. Have all vegetables cleaned and cut into bite-size pieces; hard vegetables such as cauliflower, carrots, and broccoli should be blanched. Arrange in one or more bowls.

To serve:

Spear the vegetable pieces on forks or skewers, dip into sauce briefly to warm and then eat. Serve with French bread slices, which can also be dunked.

Bagna Cauda II

This fine Turin version of the recipe is not as salty.

Ingredients:

2 cups (½ l) heavy cream

¼ cup (50 g) butter

8 to 10 rinsed and drained anchovy fillets

2 to 3 cloves garlic

1 white truffle

various vegetables in the amounts given in the previous recipe

How to prepare:

Bring cream to boil in a large saucepan and simmer, stirring constantly, for 15 minutes or so until volume is reduced by half. Melt butter in the fondue pot. Chop anchovies and garlic finely and sauté lightly in the butter; do not brown. Add the cream and the very thinly sliced truffle (a black truffle or 2 soaked, finely chopped dried mushrooms will do as a substitute). Stir constantly until mixture just begins to bubble; do not boil. Dip vegetables as described in previous recipe.

Hint:

If the sauce should separate at the table, beat it briskly until smooth with a whisk.

From Around the World

Okaribayaki

This Japanese recipe could be described as a kind of dry sukiyaki, traditionally eaten by hunters in Japan. We like to cook this outdoors in the summer over a charcoal fire, or any time of the year in a heavy iron pan set over a burner.

Ingredients:

1 duckling (about 4 pounds or 2 kg)

3 to 4 egg whites

monosodium glutamate

4 dried Japanese mushrooms (shiitake)

½ cup (⅛ l) soy sauce

1 bell pepper

1 canned sweet potato

1 white radish

1 small piece cucumber

1 egg yolk

salt

oil

How to prepare:

Cut up the duckling and remove the two breast pieces. Cut breasts into thin slices. Remove the skin from the remaining duck, cut it into strips, and fry until crisp in a skillet. Remove the remaining meat from the bones and grind finely. Beat the ground duck with the egg whites and a pinch of monosodium glutamate and let stand 10 minutes. Shape into ½-inch balls. Soak the mushrooms for 30 minutes, pour off water, discard stems and cut caps into strips. Beat the soy sauce with a pinch of monosodium glutamate and pour into a bowl. Seed pepper and cut into thin strips; cut the sweet potato into thin slices.

Arrange the duck meat, the meatballs, mushrooms, pepper strips, and potato slices on a platter. Grate the radish and cucumber and mix with the egg yolk, salt and some monosodium glutamate. Divide this dip among small bowls and place before each guest. Oil the pan well and place on burner—or first heat in kitchen—and heat until very hot. Give each diner a skewer or fondue fork.

To serve:

Each guest takes a few different items and dips them into soy sauce, then fries them in the pan. After frying, the food is cooled in the radish dip. The crisp duck skin is nibbled in between.

Tunkis

This is a rustic potato dish that we ate in the Black Forest many years ago, when fondue was still unknown to us. For the best potatoes to use, see the introduction to the recipe for Fondue Ranchero on page 87.

Ingredients:

4 large onions

2 tablespoons (3 cl) wine vinegar

3 tablespoons (5 cl) oil

freshly ground pepper

salt

hot, cooked unpeeled potatoes

How to prepare:

Slice the onions thinly. Mix with vinegar, oil, pepper, and salt. Place into a bowl and set in the middle of the table. Dip in potatoes and use them to scoop up the onions.

Klever's Tunkis

Our name for this variation of the basic recipe.

Ingredients:

1 pound 10 ounces (750 g) sieved cottage cheese

2 eggs

¼ *cup (6 cl) oil*

1 tablespoon finely chopped chives

salt

freshly ground pepper

pinch of sugar

hot, cooked unpeeled potatoes

How to prepare:

Mix the cottage cheese, beaten eggs, oil, chives, and seasonings until smooth and creamy. Place into a bowl.

To serve:

Dunk with potatoes. With this serve browned butter, chopped fresh herbs of all kinds, coarse salt, and small pieces of Camembert cheese.

Best with Dips

Artichoke Fondue

This and the following recipes come alive with varied dips and sauces.

Ingredients:

For each person:

2 artichokes

½ lemon

salt

How to prepare:

Wash the artichokes and tear away tough outer leaves (do not cut off the tips of the remaining leaves). Trim off the stem and the bottom 3 or 4 leaves. Rub the cut surface with lemon. Cook the artichokes in boiling salted water to which a little lemon juice has been added; they are done when a leaf can be pulled off easily, which will take about 45 minutes. Drain artichokes upside down. Serve warm or cold. They are eaten with the fingers, pulling the leaves off one by one. Dip the bottom, thicker portion of each leaf in the sauce and scrape off the pulp with the teeth. Have large plates ready for the scraped leaves. Don't forget a fork, with which you can remove the fibrous choke and then cut the best part—the bottom—into pieces to dip into the sauce.

To serve:

We use prepared sauces, mayonnaise thinned with plain yogurt, remoulade, vinaigrette, Herb Sauce (see recipe, page 110), Breton Sauce (page 106), Nizza Sauce (page 112), Roquefort Sauce (page 116), Warm Devil's Sauce (page 118), Gribiche Sauce (page 109), and Maltese Sauce (page 111).

Asparagus Fondue

Buy thick asparagus. If you are not planning to cook them soon after purchase, store them up to two days wrapped in a damp towel. And be careful; it is easy to overcook them.

Ingredients:

For each person:

2 pounds (1 kg) asparagus

salt (1 tablespoon per 8 cups or 2 l of water)

pinch of sugar

How to prepare:

Cut off the tough ends, then peel the asparagus from below the tip down to the end; reserve peelings. Wash asparagus briefly. Place the asparagus peelings in a pot, add salt and water and cook for 15 minutes. Add sugar and the bundled and tied asparagus, making sure they are covered with boiling water. Cook for 10 to 15 minutes, depending on thickness; test the thickest part to make sure they are tender. (For even cooking, all the asparagus should be the same thickness.) Drain asparagus and serve warm, a few at a time.

90

To serve:

We serve melted browned butter, firm butter in thin slices, soft herb butter, eggs (soft-boiled, scrambled, fried, or hard-boiled and chopped or halved), and various kinds of ham—air-dried, boiled or smoked, cut either thick or thin. Prosciutto, smoked meats, sliced beef brisket, smoked goose, and thinly sliced smoked port are all good accompaniments. You can add shrimp, lobster or crayfish tails, or smoked salmon for elegance; Spanish mussels, preserved in oil, add a piquant note. For dipping try mayonnaise—plain, or blended with whipped cream, plain yogurt, or garlic (don't worry, asparagus kills the odor of garlic). Also excellent are Hollandaise Sauce (see recipe, page 110), Tarragon Sauce (page 117), Chantilly Sauce (page 106), or Hazelnut Sauce (page 109).

Hint:

If you have a special asparagus cooker, cook the asparagus trimmings, then remove them, add the bundled asparagus in its removable rack, and cook until done.

Mustard Fondue

The fun of this fondue is the variety of mustards: there should be up to 12. When you go through the gourmet section of your market, you will find many mustards from other countries, especially French ones.

Ingredients:

For 5 persons:

12 bratwurst

6 bockwurst

12 cocktail frankfurters

6 veal sausages

6 frankfurters

6 knockwurst

1 pound (450 g) kielbasa

a cheese platter of Emmentaler, Edam, Gruyère, and Gouda

1 pound (450 g) cooked bacon

1 pound (450 g) head cheese

1 pound (450 g) pickled pigs' feet

at least 1 jar each grainy mustard, horseradish mustard, hot mustard, herb mustard, homemade mustard, and sweet mustard

a variety of peasant breads, pretzels, rolls

To serve:

In the middle of the table place a large pot or soup tureen of hot water containing the hot, cooked sausages, along with the cheese platter, bacon, head cheese, pigs' feet, and mustards. Serve with beer and clear brandies. This will be an extended feast during which everyone talks only of food.

91

Sour Sausages

Ingredients:

3 cups (¾ l) water

3 tablespoons (5 cl) wine vinegar

2 teaspoons sugar

½ teaspoon salt

1 bay leaf

2 large onions

24 small bratwurst

How to prepare:

Bring water with vinegar, sugar, salt, and bay leaf to a boil. Cut the onions into very thin slices, place in broth, and cook until soft. Add the wurst to the boiling water and simmer 15 minutes. Serve in broth with onions.

Pan Fondue

What we call a meal in which everyone—guests or just the family—has a small individual skillet that he places on the burner. Each person has a pan, a wooden board on which he can rest it, and a plate. This one may be more fun than any other fondue.

What to fry in this little pan? Steaks and thin, small slices of meat of all kinds. Lamb steaks, veal medallions, tournedos, and the like are also suitable. They are fried dry (if the pans have a nonstick coating) or in a little butter.

Other meat possibilities: Veal or pork liver slices, pieces of chicken liver, bacon slices rolled with sage leaves, thin slices of veal kidney, turkey or chicken breast slices, small meatballs or mini beef burgers, small bratwurst, thin slices of bologna, boiled ham.

What else can be fried? Thick slices of Appenzeller or Emmentaler cheese melted to make a sort of Raclette. Fry eggs, or scramble them and flavor with herbs, cubes of ham, or cheese. Mushrooms, which have been thinly sliced, soaked in water with lemon juice, drained, and patted dry. Eggplant, zucchini, and cucumbers, thinly sliced. Thick slices of orange with the skin, bananas halved lengthwise, apple slices, and pineapple rings, sprinkled with sugar to caramelize.

Accompaniments:

Salt (fine and coarse, if possible), seasoned salt, pepper mill or coarsely ground pepper, different kinds of dried herbs in their jars, curry powder, ketchups, relishes. Different kinds of bread, potato chips with a variety of seasonings. Salads, pearl onions, cornichons. You will marvel at the cooking talents you discover in your guests. Add whiskey and Cognac, and perhaps one of your guests will experiment with a flambé.

Fondue Around a Grill

The whole range of meats, vegetables, and fruit that are to be found in the pan fondue can also be used in mini-grills, which are cooked at table beautifully.

Diablotins

Ingredients:

6 round, ½-inch-thick slices white bread

4 ounces (120 g) Roquefort cheese

2 ounces (50 g) ground walnuts

2 ounces (50 g) butter

freshly ground white pepper

How to prepare:

Lightly toast bread in toaster or on tabletop grill. Mix the cheese, nuts, butter, and white pepper and place into a bowl for self-service at the table. Each one spreads his own warm toast and grills it 2 to 3 minutes. The taste of nuts and sharp cheese is heavenly.

To serve:

Eat while warm with some cranberry-orange relish to tone down the flavor. With this drink a light beer or a hearty red wine.

A hibachi-type charcoal grill is excellent for an outdoor fondue around a grill. Made of heavy cast iron, it is compact and has excellent ventilation, which keeps it from smoking as heavily as other grills of this type.

On a Skewer

All kinds of skewered foods, called *lamchi* and *boonchi* in the Antilles and *sate* in Indonesia, are broiled. Here are the recipes.

Lamchi and Boonchi

These skewers should be grilled in the garden or on the terrace or balcony.

Ingredients:

Marinade for 4 skewers:

Juice of 2 limes

2 tablespoons (3 cl) olive oil

1 onion

1 hot pepper

1 teaspoon curry powder

2 teaspoons ground ginger

2 teaspoons turmeric

1 teaspoon salt

1 clove garlic

Skewers:

16 2-inch cubes lamb shoulder

2 slices pineapple (fresh, if possible), cut in pieces

4 slices bacon

8 strips green bell pepper, 2 inches long

How to prepare:

For the marinade, mix the lime juice with the olive oil and chopped onion. Seed the hot pepper, chop finely, and add to liquid with the spices, salt, and pressed garlic. Place the meat into marinade, turning to coat all sides, and marinate overnight. Spear the lamb on skewers, alternating with pineapple pieces, rolled bacon slices and pepper strips. Each diner grills his own skewer, brushing with marinade now and then. Distance from the coals should be about 4 inches; cooking time, according to taste, will be about 10 to 15 minutes.

To serve:

Eat with Peanut Sauce (see recipe, page 115).

Sate Ajam Chicken Skewers

Ingredients:

4 whole boned chicken breasts with skin

fresh lemon juice

salt

freshly ground pepper

How to prepare:

Cut the raw meat into 1-inch cubes. Spear 5 of these cubes on each wooden skewer, sprinkle with lemon juice and season with salt and pepper. Let stand 15 minutes. Grill 10 minutes over hot coals. Serve with a variety of sauces and dips, both homemade and the Indonesian sauces found in Oriental markets.

Variations:

Instead of chicken, use 8 ounces (225 g) lamb, beef, or pork per person. The meat should be lean and only from quick-cooking cuts.

Tip:

The meat (whichever kind is used) can be marinated before grilling. Here are two marinades to choose from:

Marinade I

Ingredients:

1 teaspoon ground caraway seed

1 teaspoon ground coriander

1 teaspoon minced garlic

1 tablespoon brown sugar

2 tablespoons (3 cl) sweet soy sauce (kecap manis)

1 tablespoon fresh lemon or lime juice

salt

3 drops Tabasco

How to prepare:

Mix all ingredients and let meat cubes marinate for a few hours. Do not brush with marinade while grilling.

Marinade II

Ingredients:

1 tablespoon grated onion

1 tablespoon chopped garlic

1 tablespoon ground coriander

1 tablespoon curry powder

5 tablespoons grated coconut

1/2 cup (1/8 l) clear beef broth

2 tablespoons (3 cl) fresh lemon or lime juice

2 tablespoons brown sugar

salt

freshly ground pepper

How to prepare:

Mix all the ingredients with the cubes of meat in a pot. Bring to a boil and stew for 10 minutes. Spear the cooled cubes on skewers and serve for grilling. They should be grilled on all sides for 8 minutes.

Stone Age Fondue

The Japanese have recently introduced a piece of equipment that reminds us of ancient times: everything is cooked on a larger-than-dinner-plate-size stone platter.

Japanese Stone Fondue

Picture on page 96

Ingredients

1¾ to 2¼ pounds (750 to 1000 g) pork fillets (2 to 3 whole fillets)

For the marinade:

2 tablespoons sesame seed

2 cloves garlic

1 small onion

2 tablespoons (3 cl) peanut oil or melted butter

5 tablespoons (8 cl) sweet soy sauce (kecap manis)

1/2 cup (1/8 l) chicken broth (can be made from cubes)

How to prepare:

Skin the pork fillets and cut into ¼-inch-thick medallions. Toast the sesame seed in a dry skillet until light brown, stirring constantly. Remove from pan and cool. Chop the garlic and onion coarsely. Puree the sesame, garlic, onion, oil, soy sauce, and chicken broth in blender. Pour over medallions, turn to coat, and marinate for a few hours. Drain, reserving marinade. Dry the meat slices. Heat the stone plate on a burner until very hot. Brush with peanut oil. Have each person fry his meat slices until well done, about 8 to 10 minutes.

To serve:

Eat with French bread (see recipe, page 129), and dip in Peanut Sauce, Lime Dip and Calcutta Dip (pages 115, 121, 119).

Variation:

1¾ pounds (800 g) beef filet, in paper-thin slices, some scallions, halved and cut into bite-size pieces, 2 leeks and 2 carrots cut into thin slices (the round carrot slices can be trimmed into squares if desired). Fry on the stone plate as directed. With this serve Peanut Sauce (see recipe, page 115) or a sauce made of 1 cup (¼ l) soy sauce cooked briefly with ½ cup (1/8 l) rice wine and flavored with the juice of 2 lemons, about ½ teaspoon each salt and sugar and about 1 teaspoon finely chopped chives.

94

In 1966 the first sweet fondue was developed in New York; it is the Toblerone Fondue, recipe on page 97.

SWEET TREATS

Dessert Fondues

We will begin with an interesting cooking story. In 1966 about 100 journalists were invited to a press conference with food served afterwards. For the first course there was a cheese fondue, the second course was a meat fondue *Bourguignonne,* and the third course was a surprise—a Toblerone chocolate fondue. In a ceramic pot over a candle flame bubbled melted Toblerone. There were small forks and a choice of bread cubes, broken cookies, and fruit pieces to spear and dip into the chocolate cream.

Many newspapers and magazines commented on the new dessert, and it conquered the American continent. The director of the largest Swiss restaurant in New York was skeptical, calling it nonsense. But he tried it and put it on the menu, and his customers were enchanted. Then the Plaza Hotel added the Toblerone Fondue to the menu—and it triumphed.

In 1967 the dessert came to Switzerland—where it was served in the winter resorts of Gstaad, Grindelwald and Verbier—and then to Germany, where it is known simply as *Schokoladenfondue* without mention of the brand of chocolate. But we must say that this fondue tastes better when made with Toblerone. The honey and almond mixture of this special chocolate really makes it superb.

Naturally the chocolate mixture led our thoughts to more sweet dessert fondues. One of our biggest hits has been a coffee fondue, which of course is included here. There are also several suggestions for birthday party fondues requiring little preparation, and for novel ice cream desserts.

Toblerone Fondue

Picture on page 95

Ingredients:

½ cup (⅛ l) heavy cream

3 bars Toblerone, each 4 ounces (100 g)

1 tablespoon Cognac, rum, or milk

Outstanding and new, the Japanese Stone Fondue involves frying and dipping foods in a stone plate—recipe on page 94.

How to prepare:

Warm the cream in a small saucepan. Break chocolate into pieces, add to the cream and stir until melted. Thin slightly with Cognac, being careful that it does not ignite. Pour into small fondue pot and place over a candle warmer.

To serve:

This tastes best with white bread or cake cubes, pieces of pear or apple, banana slices, cherries, mandarin orange sections, or grapes. Also good are wholewheat bread or Snacks (see recipe, page 128), sprinkled with a few drops of rum.

Note:

We find bread or Blini (see recipe, page 130) the best dippers because then the mixture is not excessively sweet.

American Variations:

Instead of rum, use coffee liqueur. Or use 1 tablespoon each of Cognac, Cointreau, peppermint liqueur and instant coffee powder. Into these variations, dip marshmallows, banana cubes, and pieces of dried apricot.

Whiskey Chocolate Fondue

Ingredients:

1 cup (¼ l) heavy cream

4 ounces (120 g) unsweetened chocolate

4 ounces (120 g) milk chocolate

1 tablespoon instant coffee powder

1 tablespoon Scotch whiskey

How to prepare:

Warm the cream and add chocolate, broken into small pieces. Stir constantly over low heat until melted. Dissolve coffee in whiskey and stir into chocolate. Place over a candle warmer.

To serve:

Serve with wholewheat bread, Blini (see recipe, page 130), or well-drained pineapple chunks.

Chocolate Fondue with Nuts

Ingredients:

1 cup (¼ l) heavy cream

8 ounces (225 g) milk chocolate with nuts

2 tablespoons (3 cl) Cognac

pinch of ground coriander

How to prepare:

Warm the cream and add the chocolate, broken into small pieces. Stir over low heat until melted. Stir in Cognac and coriander.

To serve:

Have ready for dipping wholewheat bread, honey cake cubes, and pieces of apple. The nuts can be spooned out of the pot at the end.

Chocolate Fondue Jamaica

Ingredients:

½ cup (⅛ l) heavy cream

8 ounces (200 g) Tobler chocolate with rum

2 tablespoons (3 cl) white rum

How to prepare:

Warm the cream and add the chocolate, broken into small pieces. Stir over low heat until melted. Stir in rum. Place over a candle warmer.

To serve:

Dip pound cake cubes, sliced figs, ladyfingers, or Oatmeal Bread (see recipe, page 128). The raisins and nuts in the Tobler bar can be spooned out of the pot at the end.

98

Perfumed Chocolate Fondue

Ingredients:

1 cup (¼ l) heavy cream

8 ounces (225 g) semisweet chocolate

2 tablespoons (3 cl) quince jelly

1 tablespoon rum

How to prepare:

Warm the cream and add the chocolate, broken into small pieces. Add the jelly and stir until all is melted. Perfume with the rum.

To serve:

Dip halved, firm-fleshed prune plums, blue grapes, apple pieces, and white bread.

Variations:

Instead of quince jelly and rum, use bitter orange marmalade and whiskey, or currant jelly and kirsch, or lemon jelly and Cognac, or sour cherry marmalade and cherry brandy.

Mint Chocolate Fondue

Ingredients:

½ cup (⅛ l) heavy cream

2 tablespoons (3 cl) peppermint liqueur

8 ounces (225 g) semisweet chocolate

How to prepare:

Warm the cream and add the liqueur. Grate the chocolate coarsely, add to cream, and stir until melted. Place on a candle warmer.

To serve:

When you want something very sweet and do not have to count calories, dip bite-size pieces of candied

fruit. Also good are bite-size pieces of firm fresh or canned pear, white bread or pound cake cubes.

Tips:

If you serve a chocolate fondue for Christmas, dip with cubes of stollen. Experiment with the different liqueurs to flavor chocolate fondue. Leave out the brandies for children (even though the alcohol is cooked away before the dipping starts). Watch out that the fondue does not burn or become too thick. If necessary, thin it with a little water, strong coffee, cream, or Cognac.

Note:

There is really no wine that goes well with chocolate fondue. If you like, serve glasses of milk or cups of strong coffee. If the sweetness is a little too much, serve with water or mineral water, or a glass of Cognac or rum.

Sauce Fondue

Next, a fondue which will appeal to all those who love to dunk their bread in coffee. We call this "Double Dip."

Ingredients:

4 cups (1 l) hot, strong coffee

4 slices pound cake

heavy cream

crème de cacao

sugar

cinnamon

12 bite-size unfilled cream puffs

How to prepare:

Serve the hot coffee in large cups. Everyone gets a cup of coffee, a spoon and a fondue fork. Cut the cake into bite-size pieces. Season the coffee according to your taste with cream, crème de cacao, sugar, and cinnamon. Spear a piece of cake or cream puff and dunk until soaked with coffee. In between, drink a swallow of coffee.

Variation:

This can also be made with espresso.

Royal Mocha Fondue

An American modification of the previous recipe.

Ingredients:

8 ounces (225 g) semisweet chocolate

1/2 cup (1/8 l) hot strong coffee

3 tablespoons (5 cl) heavy cream

3 tablespoons (5 cl) Cognac

pinch of ground cinnamon

How to prepare:

Break chocolate into small pieces and melt in the coffee, stirring with a wooden spoon until creamy. Stir in cream, Cognac, and cinnamon.

To serve:

Serve with marshmallows, cubes of pound cake, or slices of peach.

Marshmallow Fondue

This fondue is appropriate for a child's birthday. For a big group, prepare a double amount.

Ingredients:

5 ounces (150 g) marshmallows

2 tablespoons (3 cl) fresh lemon juice

water

1/2 cup (1/8 l) heavy cream

How to prepare:

Melt the marshmallows with the lemon juice and a little water over medium heat. Stir in cream until smooth.

To serve:

Use pineapple slices, peach slices, and cake cubes for dipping.

Butter Nut Fondue

Ingredients:

2 cups (1/2 l) prepared butterscotch sauce

1/2 cup (1/8 l) heavy cream

1/2 cup (50 g) chopped pecans

1 large can pear halves or apricot halves

5 ounces (150 g) marshmallows

How to prepare:

Heat the sauce, cream, and nuts in a fondue pot until creamy; keep hot, but do not boil. Cut the fruits into cubes and dip in the cream. Marshmallows are best speared on wooden skewers or long toothpicks.

Hint:

This is a lightning-quick fondue that tastes every bit as good as the previous one.

Butter Rum Fondue

Prepare your favorite pancakes for dipping, or use our Blini recipe.

Ingredients:

1/2 cup (100 g) firmly packed brown sugar

1/4 cup (50 g) butter

2 egg yolks

1/4 cup (6 cl) dark Jamaica rum

8 small pancakes or Blini (see recipe, page 130)

How to prepare:

Melt the sugar and butter, stirring constantly, in the fondue pot. Remove from heat and beat in egg yolks and rum. Stir over lowest heat or a candle warmer until creamy. Prepare the pancakes, roll up, and cut into strips. Holding strips with wooden skewers or fondue forks, dip in the rum, sugar, and butter sauce.

Caramel Fondue

Ingredients:

8 ounces (225 g) cream caramels

½ cup (⅛ l) heavy cream or water

1 tablespoon rum

How to prepare:

Melt the caramels in the cream, stirring constantly over low heat. Add the rum. Keep warm.

To serve:

Dip apple pieces, walnuts (which are hard to spear, but taste good), macaroons, and banana pieces.

Sweet Tooth Fruit Fondue

Ingredients:

juice of 6 lemons

juice of 6 oranges

¼ cup (6 cl) confectioners sugar or honey

How to prepare:

Mix the fruit juices and sweeten with sugar or honey. Simmer 5 minutes in fondue pot.

To serve:

Use orange sections, peach slices, pineapple pieces, melon balls, pitted cherries, pitted dates, pieces of fig, kiwi slices, drained canned lychees—or whatever fruit is interesting.

Hints:

Serve fruits at room temperature. Dip with wooden skewers in warm sauce.

Curried Fruit Fondue

Ingredients:

1 cup (¼ l) chicken broth

1 cup (¼ l) Marsala

1 tablespoon curry powder

1 tablespoon arrowroot

1 tablespoon cold water

How to prepare:

Cook broth, wine, and curry together for 10 minutes. When the liquid is heated through and well blended, and the curry is completely dissolved, pour into fondue pot. Mix the arrowroot with water, add to broth mixture and boil briefly until thickened and clear.

To serve:

Use fruits as in Sweet Tooth Fruit Fondue above, as well as cubes of avocado. All fruit pieces should be frozen until hard, then thawed 10 minutes. Serve with wooden skewers. Leave in the liquid to get hot or just warm on the outside according to your taste.

Apple Fondue

Ingredients:

1 pound 10 ounces (750 g) sour apples

1 cinnamon stick

1 long strip lemon peel

2 cups (½ l) water

1 tablespoon butter

1 tablespoon flour

2 cups (½ l) wine

3 to 4 tablespoons sugar

1 teaspoon cornstarch (optional)

How to prepare:

Peel and quarter apples and cook with cinnamon and lemon peel in water until soft. Sieve. Melt the butter and sauté flour until golden. Slowly stir in wine and sugar; do not boil, but just stir until sugar is dissolved. Stir in apple puree and heat again. If the apple fondue is too thin, stir in cornstarch mixed with a little water. Place on burner set on the lowest flame or on candle warmer.

To serve:

Dunk with Snacks (see recipe, page 128) or pumpernickel and walnuts.

Note:

If you are in a hurry, cider or apple wine thickened with flour can be substituted for apple puree.

102

Sour Cherry Ice Cream Fondue

Ingredients:

1/3 cup (75 g) sugar

1/4 cup sliced almonds

1 pound 10 ounces (750 g) canned pitted sour cherries

2 to 3 teaspoons cornstarch

2 tablespoons (3 cl) rum or brandy

For each person:

2 canned pear halves

2 canned peach halves

crushed ice

1/2 pint (1/4 l) vanilla ice cream, frozen hard

How to prepare:

Caramelize the sugar in a heavy pan, stirring until melted and golden brown. Add almonds and brown. Drain cherries, reserving juice, and puree half in blender. Heat the puree with remaining cherries and reserved juice, saving 1/4 cup (6 cl) of the juice. Mix the cornstarch with the 1/4 cup juice. Add to fondue and cook until thick. Add the caramelized almonds. Set over a tabletop burner and perfume with rum. Cut the canned fruits into bite-size pieces and divide into portions. Divide crushed ice among 4 soup plates. Dice the ice cream, place in chilled individual bowls, and set them on ice. Serve at once, dipping fruit and ice cream cubes.

Caramel Ice Cream Fondue

Ingredients:

8 ounces (225 g) cream toffee

7 tablespoons (10 cl) water

1 ounce (30 g) walnuts

2 tablespoons (3 cl) rum or arrak

How to prepare:

Bring the toffee and water to a boil and stir until melted, about 10 minutes. Finely chop walnuts. Set the fondue on a burner and stir in nuts and rum.

To serve:

Dip pieces of fruit and ice cream cubes as for Sour Cherry Ice Cream Fondue. These ice cream fondues must be planned ahead so that you will have enough ice. Transfer the finished ice cubes to a plastic bag in the freezer while the next batch freezes.

Simple Ice Cream Fondue

This is a fondue for people in a hurry; it is not cooked, and it needs no burner, only a variety of bowls for prepared sauces.

Ingredients:

½ cup (⅛ l) strawberry sauce

½ cup (⅛ l) raspberry sauce

½ cup (⅛ l) cherry sauce

½ cup (⅛ l) blueberry sauce

½ cup (⅛ l) chocolate sauce

For each person:

8 ounces (225 g) fresh fruits of the season
    (strawberries, raspberries, apricots, peaches)

½ pint vanilla ice cream, frozen hard

How to prepare:

Place the various sauces in small bowls. Peel fruit and cut into bite-size pieces. Arrange vanilla ice cream as in Sour Cherry Ice Cream Fondue (page 102) and serve fruits and ice cream quickly for dunking.

Sauces, Dips, and Condiments

Except for cheese fondues, where the cheese mixture is its own sauce, dipping sauces are an indispensable part of a fondue meal. There should be a large number of sauces for a meat or fish fondue, since personal choice and variety are important to the fondue ritual.

Along with sauces there are also dips, usually based on cottage cheese, cream cheese, or sour cream. There are great numbers of dip recipe variations, particularly American ones.

We have included a number of sauces and dips for you. There are classic recipes and simple new discoveries; all are easy to make. Then, of course, there are also dozens of commercial sauces to choose from. The most familiar of these prepared sauces is tomato ketchup, which gives flavor to a variety of tasty recipes but is not as good as the special sauces when used alone.

Prepared packaged sauces should be served in their bottles or jars; to fill small bowls and pass them as your own creations is culinary fraud. Naturally they can be used as a basis for a dip, or can be altered through small additions as we do in many of the following recipes. These can legitimately be served in bowls.

Sauces

Aioli

Here is a classic Provençal sauce.

Ingredients:

4 cloves garlic

½ teaspoon salt

1 egg yolk

1 cup (¼ l) olive oil

fresh lemon juice

How to prepare:

Work with a mortar and pestle or a food processor. Crush the garlic with salt until mashed. Add egg yolk and blend in oil drop by drop. When mixture is the thickness of mayonnaise, flavor to taste with lemon juice.

Especially good with:

Fish Fondue; Artichoke and Asparagus Fondue.

Variations:

Stir in 3 finely chopped cloves garlic. Sharpen the taste with 2 drops Tabasco.

Anchovy Sauce I

Ingredients:

¼ cup (6 cl) mayonnaise

¼ cup (6 cl) heavy cream

8 anchovy fillets or 1 tablespoon anchovy paste

2 tablespoons chopped chives

1 teaspoon Tabasco

2 teaspoons Cognac or brandy

How to prepare:

Mix mayonnaise and cream. Chop anchovy fillets and mash into a paste, or substitute anchovy paste. Blend with chives, Tabasco, Cognac, and mayonnaise mixture.

Especially good with:

Meat Fondues cooked in oil.

Anchovy Sauce II

Ingredients:

2 small tubes anchovy paste

juice of 1 lemon or lime

1/2 cup (1/8 l) heavy cream

pinch of sugar

How to prepare:

Mix the anchovy paste with lemon juice and cream, and sweeten with sugar. Serve in 4 hollowed-out lemon halves.

Especially good with:

Nouvelle Cuisine Fondues and Seafood Fondues.

Applesauce

Ingredients:

1/2 cup (1/8 l) sour cream

3 tablespoons (5 cl) sharp Dijon mustard

1/2 onion

2 apples

salt

freshly ground pepper

2 hard-cooked eggs

How to prepare:

Mix the sour cream and mustard. Grate the onion into the mixture. Season with salt and pepper. Chop eggs and stir in.

Especially good with:

Boiled Meat Fondue; Seafood Fondues; grilled foods.

Variations:

Season with 1 teaspoon curry powder to make sauce ideal for Seafood and Lamb Fondues. This makes an interesting seafood cocktail mixed with 8 ounces (225 g) cooked, shelled, and deveined shrimp.

105

Apricot Sauce

Ingredients:

1/2 can apricots without sugar

5 tablespoons (8 cl) mango chutney

2 tablespoons (3 cl) cider vinegar

1 teaspoon grated lemon rind

1 teaspoon sugar

How to prepare:

Mash the apricots and finely chop the chutney. Mix all ingredients in a saucepan. Stir over low heat until mixture starts to bubble.

Especially good with:

Every kind of meat, hot or cold.

Béarnaise Sauce

Ingredients:

2 tablespoons (3 cl) vinegar

1 teaspoon finely chopped fresh tarragon leaves

1 cup (225 g) Hollandaise sauce, homemade or
   purchased (see recipe, page 110)

fresh lemon juice

How to prepare:

Heat vinegar with finely chopped tarragon. Heat the
Hollandaise sauce and stir in vinegar mixture. Season with lemon juice. Serve warm.

Especially good with:

Fish Fondue; Artichoke and Asparagus Fondues.

106

Breton Sauce

Ingredients:

1 tomato

a few fresh tarragon leaves or ¼ teaspoon dried

2 tablespoons (3 cl) tomato paste

4 drops Tabasco

½ cup (120 g) mayonnaise

How to prepare:

Peel, seed, and chop tomato. Mix with remaining
ingredients.

Especially good with:

Artichoke and Asparagus Fondues.

Chantilly Sauce

Anything with "Chantilly" in its name is made with
whipped cream, which was discovered by a cook in
the Château de Chantilly.

Ingredients:

2 tablespoons (3 cl) whipped cream

6 tablespoons (9 cl) mayonnaise

1 teaspoon fresh lemon juice

freshly ground white pepper

How to prepare:

Fold cream carefully into mayonnaise. Season with
lemon juice and pepper.

Especially good with:

Meat or Fish Fondue.

Tip:

The sauce should be prepared just before serving.

China Sauce

Ingredients:

¼ cup (6 cl) mayonnaise

1 tablespoon Chinese or Indonesian soy sauce

1 hard-cooked egg

1 piece ginger

¼ cup (6 cl) stiffly beaten egg white

How to prepare:

Mix the mayonnaise and soy sauce. Chop egg;
mince ginger. Stir both into mayonnaise. Just before
serving, fold in egg whites to lighten the sauce.

Especially good with:

Chinese Fondue and all Firepots.

Coffee Butter

Ingredients:

½ cup (120 g) butter

2 ounces (60 g) cream cheese

2 tablespoons (3 cl) sharp prepared mustard

1 teaspoon instant coffee powder

How to prepare:

Mix the butter and cream cheese until well blended. Stir in mustard and coffee. Shape mixture into a roll, wrap in aluminum foil, and chill. Cut into slices and serve hot or cold, but not chilled hard.

Especially good with:

Meat and Fish Fondues.

Cold Devil's Sauce

Ingredients:

¼ cup (6 cl) tomato ketchup

3 tablespoons (5 cl) oil

1 onion

4 ounces (120 g) pimientos

1 tablespoon fresh lemon juice

sugar

salt

1 tablespoon finely chopped chives

1 tablespoon chopped parsley

few drops Worcestershire sauce

few drops Tabasco

How to prepare:

Mix the ketchup with oil. Chop onion, finely dice the pimientos and add. Season with lemon juice, sugar, and salt. Fold in herbs. Season generously with Worcestershire sauce and Tabasco.

Especially good with:

Oil- or fat-cooked Meat Fondues.

Cold Tomato Sauce

Ingredients:

1 pound (450 g) tomatoes

1 onion

1 clove garlic

1 bay leaf

1 teaspoon sugar

salt

freshly ground pepper

½ cup (⅛ l) water

½ cup (⅛ l) heavy cream

How to prepare:

Cut tomatoes into small pieces. Chop onion and garlic. Mix with bay leaf, sugar, seasonings, and water and cook for 5 minutes, then let stand for 30 minutes. Press through a sieve and cool. Fold in the lightly whipped cream.

Especially good with:

Veal Fondue, Chicken Fondue.

107

Curry Sauce I

This is low in calories.

Ingredients:

8 ounces (225 g) fine-curd cottage cheese

2 teaspoons curry powder

1 tablespoon grated apple or applesauce

salt

pinch of saffron

How to prepare:

Mix all ingredients; the pinch of saffron strengthens the color without changing the taste.

Especially good with:

Meat and Fish Fondues.

Curry Sauce II

Ingredients:

1/2 cup (120 g) mayonnaise

3 tablespoons (5 cl) evaporated milk

1 apple (about 4 ounces or 120 g)

1/2 small onion

1 to 2 teaspoons curry powder

fresh lemon juice

salt

pinch of sugar

How to prepare:

Mix mayonnaise with evaporated milk to thin. Peel and shred the apple. Stir into mayonnaise immediately to keep it from turning brown. Chop onion finely and add along with curry. Season with lemon juice, salt, and sugar.

Especially good with:

Fondue Bourguignonne.

Energy Ketchup

Ingredients:

6 ounces (180 g) tomato ketchup

2 teaspoons sweet paprika

2 tablespoons (3 cl) sour cream

1 teaspoon soy sauce

1 teaspoon cider vinegar

How to prepare:

Mix all ingredients together. Serve in a small bowl.

Especially good with:

Mustard or Meat Fondues.

Fire Sauce

Ingredients:

8 ounces (225 g) fine-curd cottage cheese

3 tablespoons (5 cl) hot ketchup

salt

freshly ground pepper

pinch of sugar

Tabasco or cayenne pepper

How to prepare:

Beat the cheese with ketchup and season with salt, pepper, and sugar. Add Tabasco or cayenne to taste.

108

Especially good with:

Meat Fondue, Cheese Fondue Bourguignonne, and Fish Kabob Fondue.

Green Asparagus Sauce

Ingredients:

1 onion

3 tablespoons (5 cl) cider vinegar

1 tablespoon asparagus cooking water

6 tablespoons (9 cl) olive oil

1 teaspoon sharp prepared mustard

1 tablespoon chopped parsley

1 tablespoon chopped raw spinach

1 tablespoon chopped watercress

½ clove garlic

How to prepare:

Chop onion fine. Mix all ingredients and stir together for 5 minutes.

Especially good with:

Asparagus or Artichoke Fondue.

Gribiche Sauce

Ingredients:

1 hard-cooked egg

1½ teaspoons finely chopped chives

1½ teaspoons finely chopped parsley

1 teaspoon (scant) chopped chervil

1 teaspoon (scant) chopped tarragon

3 cornichons

1 teaspoon capers

4 ounces (120 g) mayonnaise

How to prepare:

Separate the egg yolk and egg white. Finely chop the white; mash the yolk with a fork. Mix egg with herbs, finely chopped cornichons, capers, and mayonnaise.

Especially good with:

Artichoke, Asparagus, or Fish Fondue.

Hazelnut Sauce

Ingredients:

2 tablespoons (30 g) butter

3 tablespoons flour

1 cup (¼ l) clear beef broth or asparagus cooking water

fresh lemon juice

salt

1 egg yolk

½ cup (⅛ l) light cream or half and half

⅔ cup (100 g) hazelnuts

How to prepare:

Prepare a roux using butter, flour, and beef broth (or prepare a white sauce using a packaged white sauce mix). Season with lemon juice and salt. Beat egg yolk and cream and stir into sauce. Toast the hazelnuts in a skillet, rub off skins, and chop. Stir hazelnuts into sauce.

Especially good with:

Fish Fondue, Asparagus Fondue.

109

Herb Sauce

Ingredients:

1 tablespoon chopped chervil

1 tablespoon chopped parsley

1 tablespoon finely chopped chives

1½ teaspoons chopped tarragon

1 cup mayonnaise

How to prepare:

Mix the fresh herbs with mayonnaise and serve at once.

Especially good with:

Fish Skewer Fondue; Artichoke or Asparagus Fondue.

Tip:

If necessary, use 1 teaspoon dried herbs instead of 1 tablespoon fresh. Finely crush the herbs in your hand, then let stand in mayonnaise for 15 to 30 minutes to allow flavor to develop.

Hollandaise Sauce

Ingredients:

2 tablespoons (3 cl) wine vinegar

1½ teaspoons finely chopped onion

4 to 6 peppercorns

1 to 2 tablespoons water

3 egg yolks

1 cup (225 g) butter

fines herbs

fresh lemon juice

How to prepare:

Combine the vinegar, chopped onion, and crushed peppercorns in a small saucepan and bring to a boil. Add cold water and press through a sieve. Add egg yolks, place mixture in a double boiler top set over simmering water, and beat constantly until a thick cream. Melt the butter (it should be warm, not hot). Beating constantly, add the butter to the sauce a drop at a time. Season to taste with fines herbes and lemon juice. If the sauce is too thick, add a little water.

Especially good with:

Chinese Fondue, all Fish and Seafood Fondues, and Asparagus and Artichoke Fondues.

Variations:

Sauce Mousseline (and also the genuine Sauce Chantilly) is made from Hollandaise. Fold 4 heaping tablespoons of whipped cream into 2 cups Hollandaise.

Honey Dip

Ingredients:

8 ounces (225 g) seedless raisins

½ cup (⅛ l) water

2 tablespoons (3 cl) honey

2 tablespoons (3 cl) hot ketchup

1 tablespoon soy sauce

salt

4 drops Tabasco

dash or Worcestershire sauce

How to prepare:

Process raisins and water in blender until pureed. Stir in honey and remaining ingredients. (These can be varied—it's the raisin and honey mixture that is most important.)

110

Especially good with:

Fondue Bourguignonne.

Horseradish Sauce

Ingredients:

1 onion

1 apple

1 tablespoon oil

½ cup (⅛ l) water

½ cup (⅛ l) milk

1 envelope white sauce mix

1 egg yolk

3 tablespoons (5 cl) grated fresh or 1 tablespoon dried horseradish

½ teaspoon horseradish mustard

salt

pinch of sugar

2 tablespoons (3 cl) stiffly whipped cream

How to prepare:

Peel onion and apple, grate finely, and brown in oil. Stir in water, milk, and sauce mix and stir until thick. Beat in egg yolk and season with horseradish and remaining seasonings. Fold in whipped cream.

Especially good with:

Boiled Meat Fondue.

Indonesian Sauce

Ingredients:

¼ cup (60 g) butter

½ cup (⅛ l) Indonesian soy sauce

2 tablespoons (3 cl) fresh lemon juice

salt

freshly ground pepper

1 bottled hot pepper

How to prepare:

Melt butter. Add the soy sauce, lemon juice, salt, and pepper. Cut open the hot pepper, remove seeds, and chop the pod. Add to sauce, bring to a boil and simmer 2 minutes.

Especially good with:

Indonesian Meat Skewers.

Variations:

Instead of the butter use peanut butter. At the end, stir in 1 tablespoon instant minced onion.

111

Maltese Sauce

Ingredients

2 tablespoons (3 cl) wine vinegar

1½ teaspoons chopped sweet onion

4 peppercorns

¼ cup (6 cl) orange juice

3 egg yolks

1 cup (225 g) butter

fines herbes

1 tablespoon slivered orange rind

How to prepare:

Bring the vinegar, onion, and peppercorns to a boil. Add 2 tablespoons (3 cl) of the orange juice and strain the sauce through a sieve. Beat in the egg yolks. Transfer mixture to a double boiler top set over simmering water and beat until thick and creamy. Gradually whisk in melted and cooled butter. Beat in remaining orange juice, fines herbes, and orange rind.

Especially good with:

Asparagus or Chicken Fondue.

Simple Variations:

As a substitute for Maltese Sauce, mix mayonnaise with orange juice and grated orange rind. Or beat white sauce with an egg yolk, using orange juice as part of the liquid and flavoring with grated orange rind.

Mustard Relish

Ingredients:

2 hard-cooked eggs

2 mustard pickles

3 small dill gherkins

2 pimientos

1 teaspoon capers

2 to 3 tablespoons (3 to 4 cl) pickled cocktail onions

1 bottle piccalilli sauce

coarsely ground pepper

How to prepare:

Chop eggs. Chop the mustard pickles, gherkins, pimientos, capers and onions. Combine all ingredients, seasoning with pepper.

Especially good with:

All Meat Fondues, particularly those cooked in hot oil.

Mustard Sauce

Ingredients:

2½ ounces (75 g) sharp prepared mustard

juice of 1 lemon

⅓ cup (8 cl) oil

2 teaspoons chopped parsley

12 capers

How to prepare:

Mix mustard and lemon juice, then beat gradually into oil. Stir in parsley and capers last.

Especially good with:

Chinese Fondue.

Nizza Sauce

From Nice, the French Riviera resort city.

Ingredients:

1 tablespoon tomato paste

1 cup (¼ l) plain yogurt

¼ cup (6 cl) mayonnaise

2 green bell peppers

½ teaspoon dried tarragon

salt

freshly ground pepper

How to prepare:

Mix the tomato paste with yogurt and mayonnaise. Seed peppers and grate. Stir into sauce. Add the crumbled tarragon, salt, and pepper. Chill for at least 30 minutes.

Especially good with:

All oil fondues.

Fondue is good company food; everyone eats from one pot and the mood is friendly and relaxed.

Peanut Sauce

Ingredients:

2 tablespoons (3 cl) grated onion

2 tablespoons (3 cl) olive oil

2 tablespoons flaked coconut

2/3 cup (16 cl) milk

2 tablespoons firmly packed brown sugar

1 tablespoon fresh lime or lemon juice

2 tablespoons (3 cl) peanut butter

How to prepare:

Brown the onion in oil. Soak the coconut in milk. Add the brown sugar, lime or lemon juice, and peanut butter to the onions and stir until well blended. Slowly add the milk and the soaked coconut. Stir well and cook slowly until reduced to half its volume.

Especially good with:

Fondue Around a Grill.

Peparata

Ingredients:

1/4 cup (50 g) butter or half butter, half beef marrow

1/2 cup (50 g) fine dry breadcrumbs

1/4 cup (25 g) grated Parmesan cheese

clear beef broth

salt

plenty of freshly ground pepper

How to prepare:

Melt butter in a saucepan. Stir in breadcrumbs and cheese and add enough beef broth to make a thick paste. Season with salt and pepper; the sauce should be peppery. Serve cold.

Especially good with:

Meat Fondue or Mustard Fondue with jellied meat.

Note:

This amount is for 4 persons, since only a small amount is needed per serving.

115

Potato Sauce

Another low-calorie mixture. This doesn't contain potatoes; it's eaten with them.

Ingredients:

8 ounces (225 g) fine-curd cottage cheese

4 dill pickles

1 teaspoon sweet paprika

1 tablespoon wine vinegar

1 teaspoon chopped fennel greens or chervil

milk

How to prepare:

Mix the cheese with the finely chopped pickles. Add the paprika, vinegar, and herbs. Stir well and thin with a little milk.

Especially good with:

Tunkis and Vegetable Fondues.

The firepot is very satisfying, even though the chrysanthemums are only symbolic and decorative—recipe on page 69.

Red Beet Sauce

Ingredients:

1 cup (¼ l) sour cream

3 tablespoons (5 cl) red beet juice

1 teaspoon fresh lemon juice

pinch of ground caraway seed

½ teaspoon dried dill or 1 tablespoon chopped fresh

freshly ground pepper

salt

How to prepare:

Mix all ingredients until well blended. Serve chilled.

Especially good with:

Oil- or fat-cooked Meat Fondues. Also good with herring, and with Meat Fondues cooked in broth.

Roquefort Sauce

Ingredients:

5 ounces (150 g) Roquefort cheese

½ cup (⅛ l) oil

¼ cup (6 cl) wine vinegar

salt

freshly ground pepper

How to prepare:

Mash the cheese with a fork and mix with the oil to form a paste. Make the mixture piquant with vinegar and season to taste with salt. Grind pepper over top.

Especially good with:

All kinds of Meat Fondues.

Sherry Sauce

Ingredients:

1 envelope white sauce mix

1 cup (¼ l) water

2 tablespoons (3 cl) dry Sherry

¼ cup (6 cl) stiffly whipped cream

How to prepare:

Prepare white sauce with water according to package directions. Stir in Sherry. Cool. Fold in cream. Serve cold.

Especially good with:

Punsch Fondue, Veal Skewers Bacchus, and Meatball Fondue.

Slimming Steak Sauce

Ingredients:

5 ounces (150 g) cottage cheese

5 tablespoons (8 cl) milk

1 teaspoon sharp prepared mustard

1 teaspoon grated horseradish

2 tablespoons (3 cl) rum

pinch of salt

freshly ground pepper

1 tablespoon bitter orange marmalade

How to prepare:

Mix cottage cheese and milk until smooth, then mix in remaining ingredients to make a thick sauce.

Especially good with:

Fondue Bourguignonne, Boiled Meat Fondue, and all kinds of broiled meat.

Tarragon Sauce

Ingredients:

4 egg yolks

1/2 cup (120 g) butter

salt

freshly ground white pepper

5 tablespoons (8 cl) dry white wine

1 teaspoon finely chopped fresh tarragon leaves

1 teaspoon fresh lemon juice

1/2 teaspoon sugar

How to prepare:

Beat egg yolks until foamy in heatproof bowl or double boiler top. Melt butter and gradually beat into yolks. Season with salt and pepper. Place over simmering water and continue to beat. Gradually beat in white wine, then the tarragon, lemon juice, and sugar; the sauce should be thick. Serve warm.

Especially good with:

Fish Fondues; Asparagus and Artichoke Fondues.

Tartar Sauce

Ingredients:

1 egg yolk

1 teaspoon sharp prepared mustard

fines herbes

1/2 teaspoon fresh lemon juice

about 1/2 cup (1/8 l) oil

2 onions

3 cornichons

1 tablespoon capers

1 hard-cooked egg

How to prepare:

Mix the egg yolk with mustard and fines herbes. Add lemon juice, then beat in oil a drop at a time to the consistency of mayonnaise (or substitute 1 cup prepared mayonnaise). Chop onions and cornichons and add along with capers. Chop hard-cooked egg and fold in carefully.

Especially good with:

All oil- or fat-cooked Meat Fondues; Chinese and Fish Fondues. Very good with skewered fish.

Vinaigrette

Ingredients:

1 tablespoon finely chopped parsley

2 cornichons

1 small onion

1 tablespoon sharp mustard

1/2 teaspoon capers

1 1/2 teaspoons tiny tomato cubes

2 tablespoons (3 cl) wine vinegar

1 teaspoon fines herbes

1/2 cup (1/8 l) oil

1 hard-cooked egg

How to prepare:

Mix the parsley with the finely diced cornichons, the finely copped onion, mustard, capers, and tomato cubes. Add vinegar and fines herbes. Beat in the oil until mixture forms a thick sauce. Finely chop egg and stir into sauce.

117

Especially good with:

Chinese Fondue, Boiled Meat Fondue.

Warm Devil's Sauce

Ingredients:

2 onions

1 teaspoon coarsely ground pepper

⅓ cup (8 cl) wine vinegar

⅓ cup (8 cl) very dry white wine

1 cup (¼ l) beef gravy (can be canned)

How to prepare:

Finely chop onions. Cook with pepper and vinegar until reduced to ⅓ of original volume. Add white wine and cook until reduced to ½. Press mixture through a sieve. Add gravy and reheat.

Especially good with:

Artichoke and Lamb Fondues.

Yankee Sauce

Ingredients:

2 hard-cooked eggs

1 tablespoon mild prepared mustard

salt

½ cup (⅛ l) oil

fresh lemon juice

1 tablespoon chopped cornichons

2 tablespoons chopped pearl onions

sugar

1 tablespoon grated Parmesan or other sharp cheese

How to prepare:

Remove the yolks from the halved eggs, combine with mustard, and mash them into a paste using a fork. Season with salt. Beat in oil drop by drop; add some lemon juice to keep sauce from curdling. Stir in chopped cornichons and pearl onions. Season with sugar and more salt and lemon juice if necessary. Stir in grated cheese and the finely chopped egg whites.

Especially good with:

Fish Fondues and Nouvelle Cuisine Fondue.

Dips

Apple Raisin Dip

Ingredients:

1 tablespoon seedless raisins

3 tablespoons (5 cl) red wine

1 apple

1 teaspoon fresh lemon juice

½ teaspoon Tabasco

1 tablespoon Worcestershire sauce

1 tablespoon chopped walnuts

How to prepare:

Soak raisins in red wine until they are plump. Peel and dice apple. Puree raisins, apple, lemon juice, Tabasco, and Worcestershire sauce in blender. Stir in nuts.

Especially good with:

Meat Fondue.

Avocado Dip I

Ingredients:

1 large ripe avocado

3 tablespoons (5 cl) plain yogurt

1 tablespoon mayonnaise

2 tabelspoons (3 cl) ketchup

½ teaspoon grated horseradish

1 teaspoon fresh lemon juice

1 teaspoon prepared mustard

1 tablespoon chopped capers

1 tablespoon chopped parsley

1 tablespoon chopped dill

How to prepare:

Scoop avocado flesh out of skin and combine with the yogurt, mayonnaise, ketchup, horseradish, lemon juice, and mustard in a blender or mixer. Stir in capers and herbs.

Especially good with:

Fish or Seafood Fondues.

Avocado II—Guacamole

Ingredients:

1 large ripe avocado

2 teaspoons fresh lemon or lime juice

1 teaspoon chili powder

1 clove garlic

2 tablespoons (3 cl) mayonnaise

salt

How to prepare:

Peel avocado or scoop out of the skin. Mash the pulp with a fork. Add lemon or lime juice. Stir in chili powder, crushed garlic, and mayonnaise.

Especially good with:

All Meat Fondues.

Calcutta Dip

Ingredients:

½ cup (⅛ l) heavy cream

2 packages (2 ounces each) Gervais or 4 ounces (120 g) cream cheese

3 tablespoons (5 cl) chutney

1 teaspoon curry powder

⅔ cup (120 g) cashews

How to prepare:

Whip cream until stiff. Mash the cheese and mix with the chutney and curry. Fold in whipped cream and then the finely chopped nuts.

Especially good with:

Vegetable Fondue.

Cottage Cheese Dip

Ingredients:

½ cup (⅛ l) fine-curd cottage cheese

2 freshly cooked small potatoes

1 to 2 tablespoons plain yogurt

salt

freshly ground pepper

½ teaspoon sweet paprika

1 tablespoon chopped chives

119

How to prepare:

Mix cottage cheese with the peeled, mashed potatoes. Stir in enough yogurt to make mixture creamy. Season with remaining ingredients.

Especially good with:

Meat Fondue, cooked in either oil or broth, as well as Boiled Meat Fondue.

Cranberry Horseradish Dip

Ingredients:

1 can (8 ounces or 220 g) whole berry cranberry sauce

2 tablespoons (3 cl) fresh lemon juice

2 tablespoons (3 cl) grated fresh or prepared white horseradish

How to prepare:

Mix all ingredients by hand—do not use a mixer.

Especially good with:

Meat, Game, and Variety Meat Fondues.

Garlic Cheese Dip

Ingredients:

2 to 3 cloves garlic

1 cup (225 g) mayonnaise

1 teaspoon grated Parmesan cheese

How to prepare:

Mash or press the garlic. Mix with mayonnaise and cheese.

Especially good with:

Meat or Asparagus Fondues.

Tip:

Add as much garlic as you like. Garlic powder or garlic juice can also be used.

Highland Dip

Ingredients:

5 ounces (150 g) cream cheese

milk

1 tablespoon chopped walnuts

How to prepare:

Mash the cheese until soft and creamy. Gradually beat in enough milk to make a creamy mixture. Fold in nuts.

Especially good with:

All Vegetable Fondues and skewered fish.

Horseradish Dip

Ingredients:

⅔ cup (150 g) thick sour cream

3 tablespoons (5 cl) grated fresh or 1 tablespoon dried horseradish

salt

2 drops Tabasco

2 tablespoons (3 cl) fresh lemon juice

How to prepare:

Mix all the ingredients together. The dip is fairly thin.

Especially good with:

Tunkis.

120

Variation:

Instead of sour cream, use cottage cheese and mix with some plain yogurt. Add a pinch of sugar.

Lemon Dip

Ingredients:

For 6 persons:

½ bottle chili sauce

juice of 2 lemons

grated rind of 1 lemon

How to prepare:

Mix the chili sauce with lemon juice and rind. Chill for 30 minutes in refrigerator.

Especially good with:

Meat Fondues and mixed grills.

Lime Dip

Ingredients:

5 ounces (150 g) Italian parsley

juice of 2 limes

grated rind of 1 lime

2 tablespoons (3 cl) crème fraîche or sour cream

How to prepare:

Trim tough stems from parsley and puree in blender along with lime juice and rind. Stir in crème fraîche and chill 30 minutes.

Especially good with:

All Fish Fondues.

Mushroom-Egg Dip

Ingredients:

1 can mushrooms

the same measure of chopped hard-cooked eggs

vinegar

oil

parsley

salt

coarsely ground pepper

black olives

How to prepare:

Drain mushrooms (reserving liquid) and cut into pieces. Mix in eggs. Make a marinade using vinegar, oil, some of the liquid drained from the mushrooms, and chopped parsley. Season with salt and pepper and pour over mushroom-egg mixture. Let stand for 1 hour. Garnish with black olives.

Especially good with:

Meat Fondues made with beef.

Onion Dip

Ingredients:

1 cup (¼ l) sour cream

2 tablespoons instant toasted onions

fresh lemon juice (optional)

1 large sweet onion

How to prepare:

Mix the sour cream and instant onions. If the cream is not thick enough, stir in a little lemon juice. Cut the fresh onion into paper-thin slices and stir into mixture.

121

Especially good with:

Fondue Bourguignonne and all other Meat Fondues.

Pickle Dip

Ingredients:

1 cup (¼ l) mayonnaise

1 to 2 tablespoons soy sauce

4 finely chopped dill pickles

How to prepare:

Mix all ingredients and serve at once. The pickles should be so fine that they just add a little texture.

Especially good with:

Meat Fondues made with beef.

Spanish Dip

Ingredients:

4 stuffed olives

1 anchovy fillet

2 tablespoons finely chopped green bell pepper

¼ cup (6 cl) mayonnaise

1 teaspoon grated onion

How to prepare:

Finely chop olives and anchovy. Mix with the green pepper and mayonnaise. Flavor with grated onion.

Especially good with:

Oil- or fat-cooked Meat Fondues.

Tropical Dip

Ingredients:

1 cup (225 g) mayonnaise

5 tablespoons (8 cl) tomato ketchup

2 tablespoons (3 cl) hot chili sauce

1 teaspoon dried horseradish

juice of ½ lemon

1 teaspoon sugar

How to prepare:

Mix all ingredients and season to taste. It should be sharp, but not so sharp as to mask the taste of the fondue.

Especially good with:

Oil- or fat-cooked Meat Fondues, Mustard and Meatball Fondues, and Caribbean Meatballs.

We have come to the end, even though we could write about infinitely more sauces and dips. Every evening, wherever someone eats fondue, a new dip is discovered; we venture to say that you will be inventing some, too. You have learned the basics, so now use your imagination—you may devise a great new sauce with the addition of a spoonful of whiskey or a mashed anchovy fillet. Then the best part of your fondue parties will be homemade, secret dips of your own invention. Discover!

Homemade Condiments

In the basic Fondue Bourguignonne recipe we mentioned some of the dips and sauces that can be served with any fondue cooked in oil or broth. The rule states: something spicy, something sweet-sour, something fresh, something mild, and something crisp should always be on the table. There is a great selection in supermarkets and specialty stores.

Not everyone is satisfied with buying a jar or can and just opening it. For the more ambitious cook we include here some accompaniments that are really out of the ordinary. Some—for example, the Apricot Chutney—require quite a bit of time to prepare, but these recipes are for wonderful specialties which have no counterparts in the supermarket. One accompaniment that *can* be prepared quickly is the Onions for Dipping.

With an oil or broth fondue you may wish to serve a simple salad; if so, set extra plates. It can be a green salad with herb vinaigrette; Bibb lettuce with crème fraîche-based dressing; a chicory salad with orange sections and a simple yogurt dressing; a tomato salad with paper-thin onion rings, dressed with olive oil and seasoned with salt and pepper; a cucumber salad with lemon juice, oil, and sour cream. All provide a good contrast to the grilled meat slices, broth-cooked fish pieces, or what have you. Serve only one kind of salad with each fondue.

By all means try these recipes when you want a change from dips, pearl onions and pimientos.

Apricot Chutney

Ingredients:

1 pound (450 g) dried apricots

2 cups (½ l) water

1 cup (¼ l) white wine vinegar

sugar

1 teaspoon lemon pepper

2 ounces (60 g) chopped almonds

1 tablespoon butter

2 tablespoons (3 cl) brandy

How to prepare:

Soak apricots overnight in water to cover; drain, reserving liquid. Grind the apricots through a coarse blade. Mix with vinegar and some of the soaking water. Measure and add ½ cup less sugar than fruit. Stir in lemon pepper and cook until thick, stirring frequently. Meanwhile, brown almonds in butter. At the end of the cooking time, stir the almonds and brandy into the chutney. Fill hot jelly glasses and seal.

Hint:

Don't forget to use the leftover apricots from Lamb Fondue, Syrian Style for this (see recipe, page 44).

Pineapple Pickles

Ingredients:

2 ounces (60 g) dates

¼ cup (6 cl) water

3 canned pineapple slices

2 tablespoons sugar

¼ cup (6 cl) vinegar

2 tablespoons (3 cl) pineapple juice (from can)

salt

chili powder

How to prepare:

Pit the dates and chop finely. Let soak for a few hours in ¼ cup water. Cut the pineapple slices into fine, thin segments. Mix dates and soaking water, sugar, vinegar, pineapple juice, salt, and chili powder to taste. Cook for 10 minutes, stirring constantly, then stir in pineapple pieces and cook another 5 minutes. Fill hot jelly glasses and seal. Serve cold.

Especially good with:

Meat Fondues, and any fondues with an Asian touch.

Lemon Pickles

For people who love spicy food.

Ingredients:

6 to 8 lemons or limes

1 tablespoon salt

red and green chili peppers

1 cup (¼ l) wine vinegar

How to prepare:

Wash and dry the lemons; cut each into 6 wedges. Sprinkle with salt. Arrange on racks set on cookie sheets and let lemons dry in oven set on lowest temperature (or warmed by pilot light) with the door ajar for 1 to 2 nights. Turn several times for even drying. Weigh the dried lemons and mix in ¼ of their weight in chili peppers, finely chopped (this is best done in a food processor). Transfer to a glass dish or jars, or a stoneware crock. Add vinegar and let stand in a warm place for 1 week. Skim off foam and pour off excess vinegar.

Sweet-Sour Pearl Onions

Ingredients:

12 ounces cocktail onions

3 whole cloves

1 bay leaf

piece of fresh ginger

3 cups (¾ l) white wine vinegar

1 tablespoon sugar

2 packets vanilla sugar (sold in German specialty shops)

How to prepare:

Drain onions, reserving the jars and lids in which they were packed. Grind spices coarsely; tie into a cheesecloth bag and simmer with vinegar and sugar for 10 minutes. Return onions to jars, pour hot vinegar mixture over and close immediately.

Preserved Lemons

Lemons prepared in this way are good with oil- or fat-cooked meat and fish fondues, as are mustard fruits and mixed pickles.

Ingredients:

6 lemons

20 whole cloves

10 coriander seeds

olive oil

How to prepare:

Wipe the whole lemons and place with the cloves and coriander seeds into a glass jar with a tight-fitting lid. Cover with olive oil, close and let stand 6 months, without opening or shaking. Take out only as many as you need at a time. They must always remain covered with oil.

Marinated Cherry Tomatoes

Ingredients:

1 pound (450 g) cherry tomatoes

bunch of parsley

3 sprigs fresh mint

1 celery stalk

1 small onion

1 clove garlic

10 green peppercorns

3 tablespoons (5 cl) vinegar

¼ cup (6 cl) oil

salt

Tabasco

How to prepare:

Core the tomatoes and squeeze out all seeds and juice. Coarsely chop herbs, vegetables, and garlic and place in a blender. Add the peppercorns, vinegar, and oil, and puree. Season with salt and Tabasco. Stuff into hollowed-out tomatoes and let marinate in refrigerator for at least 24 hours.

124

Homemade Sambal

Ingredients:

1 ounce (30 g) cornichons

1 small onion

2 small hot peppers

1 clove garlic

10 green peppercorns

1 ripe banana

2 tablespoons (3 cl) fresh lemon juice

2 to 3 tablespoons (3 to 4 cl) oil

salt

sugar

How to prepare:

Finely chop all the ingredients from the cornichons to the banana and mix. Stir in the lemon juice and oil. Season with salt and sugar. Chill very well. Serve the same day for dipping.

Onions for Dipping

Prepare these on the same day for an oil or vegetable fat fondue.

Ingredients:

4 large onions

2 cups (½ l) milk

1 cup (100 g) all-purpose flour

salt

freshly ground pepper

How to prepare:

Cut the onions into rings. Cover with the milk and let stand 2 to 3 hours. Drain and dry on paper tow-els. Coat with seasoned flour, shake off excess, and place into individual bowls. Fry in hot fat.

Especially good with:

All oil fondues with meat and/or vegetables.

Potato Sticks for Dipping

Ingredients:

2 pounds (1 kg) large potatoes

4 cups (1 l) oil

How to prepare:

Peel the potatoes and cut into ½-inch-thick slices, then cut slices into ½-inch strips. Pat dry with paper towels. Put small portions into the boiling oil and cook for 2 minutes or until pale brown. Drain well and cool on several thicknesses of paper towels. Place them in a large bowl near the oil fondue. Each one fries his own potato sticks, salts them, sprinkles them with paprika or dips them into a spicy sauce.

Fish Balls

Ingredients:

1 pound (450 g) cod fillets

2 egg whites

1 cup (¼ l) heavy cream

salt

freshly ground pepper

How to prepare:

Grind fish several times through a fine blade or in food processor. Beat egg whites until stiff and fold into fish. Stir in cream 1 tablespoon at a time. Season with salt and pepper. Shape into small balls. Arrange in a single layer in a large, flat pot and cover with boiling salted water. Simmer, covered, over low heat for 10 minutes. Remove with a slotted spoon and serve lukewarm or cold.

125

Especially good with:

All kinds of Chinese Fish Fondues.

Rice Flour Pancakes

This amount is enough for our Korean Beef Fondue Puegogi, for example (see recipe, page 78).

Ingredients:

1¹/₃ cups (150 g) rice flour

2 tablespoons all-purpose flour

¹/₂ teaspoon saffron

2 to 3 cups (¹/₂ to ³/₄ l) water

3 to 4 tablespoons (4 to 6 cl) oil

126

How to prepare:

Mix the flours, add saffron and mix with 2 cups (½ l) water to make a smooth dough. Let dough stand for at least 1 hour, then add more water until mixture is the consistency of regular pancake batter. Make small pancakes out of 2 tablespoons (3 cl) of the batter in a little oil. Cook carefully, as this egg-free batter bakes very quickly and the pancakes should not brown.

Note:

If you cannot obtain rice flour, the pancakes can also be made from rice: use 4 ounces (120 g) regular, not converted, rice, 2 cups (½ l) water, about 2 tablespoons all-purpose flour, ½ teaspoon saffron.

How to prepare:

Soak the rice in water overnight. Add the saffron and puree in a blender. If the batter is too thick, add more water; if too thin, add 1 to 2 tablespoons flour and blend with a mixer. Batter prepared in this way must be stirred while it is being cooked to prevent separation.

Garlic Bread

Ingredients:

French bread (see recipe, page 129)

3 cloves garlic

salt

¹/₂ cup (120 g) butter

How to prepare:

Cut the bread into slices; it will be put together again after spreading. Crush the garlic with a little salt and mix with the soft butter. Spread this garlic butter on the bread slices. Put the bread back together again, wrap in foil and bake in a preheated hot oven (400° F or 200° C) for 25 minutes.

To serve:

Serve the warm garlic bread with a meat fondue.

Home Baking Ideas

Breadbaking is fun to do, and home-baked bread is always a delightful surprise for guests—not to mention the way a loaf in the oven perfumes the whole house with its delicious aroma. Not everyone takes the trouble to bake at home and it rates real praise. Since fondue does not make for a lot of work in the kitchen, there is plenty of time for baking.

Home-baked bread is perfect for dipping in a cheese fondue—especially since, if you use a little extra yeast, the bread will have larger holes and allow cheese to soak in. And homemade bread tastes delicious when finely crumbled and covered with the broth from a Chinese fondue. Remember, too, that the crustiness of a home-baked bread can be controlled; and the crustier the bread, the better it is for fondue.

Only white bread is eaten fresh. Every other bread improves in texture and flavor if it is at least one to two days old; stored airtight, rye bread will keep a whole week.

Here now are our special baking recipes.

Rustic Sourdough Rolls

Ingredients:

2½ cups (350 g) wholewheat flour

1 tablespoon sugar

1 teaspoon baking powder

1 teaspoon salt

1 cup (200 g) sourdough starter (see recipe that follows)

½ cup (⅛ l) lukewarm water

3 tablespoons (4 cl) rendered bacon fat

¾ cup (100 g) all-purpose flour

How to prepare:

In large bowl combine wholewheat flour, sugar, baking powder, and salt. Mix well. Add sourdough starter, water, and bacon fat. Beat until well combined. Add enough of all-purpose flour to form a dough that can be kneaded. Turn out onto a floured board and knead until smooth and elastic. This will take about 8 minutes. Divide dough into 16 balls. Roll between palms of hands to produce smooth and even size. Place balls side by side in a 9-inch (23-cm) round baking pan heavily greased with bacon fat. Cover with warm, damp cloth and let rise in warm place until doubled, about 45 minutes. Bake at 400° F (200 C) for about 25 minutes, or until well browned and done. Makes 16 pull-apart rolls.

Sourdough Starter

Ingredients:

1 package (¼ ounce) active dry yeast

1 teaspoon sugar

1 cup (¼ l) lukewarm water

1 cup (125 g) all-purpose flour

How to prepare:

In large, nonmetal bowl, combine yeast, sugar, and water. Stir for 30 seconds. Add flour and beat with wooden spoon until no lumps remain. Let stand, uncovered, at room temperature for at least 2 days before using. Starter must develop a noticeably pungent sour aroma and taste. Stir down after 24 hours. After 2 days, starter may be covered and refrigerated for up to 10 days. To replenish starter, replace it with equal parts lukewarm water and all-purpose flour. For example, if you use 1 cup (200 g) starter, stir ½ cup (⅛ l) of lukewarm water and ½ cup (75 g) all-purpose flour into starter bowl.

Bacon Onion Rolls

Ingredients:

2⅔ cups (325 g) all-purpose flour

1 tablespoon sugar

½ teaspoon salt

1 package (¼ ounce) active dry yeast

⅔ cup (⅛ l) milk

¼ cup (60 g) butter

6 slices bacon

¾ cup (75 g) chopped onion

How to prepare:

In large bowl combine 2 cups (250 g) flour, sugar, salt, and yeast. Mix well. Pour milk into small saucepan over medium heat. Add butter. Cook until butter melts. Add milk mixture to dry ingredients. Beat until mixture forms a dough. Turn out onto a floured board. Knead, using additional flour, if necessary, until smooth and elastic. This will take about 8 minutes. Place dough in clean, well-greased bowl. Turn to ensure dough is coated with shortening. Cover with a warm, damp cloth. Let rise in warm place until doubled, about 45 minutes. Meanwhile, cook bacon in skillet until crisp. Remove bacon to paper towels to drain and leave rendered fat in skillet. Add chopped onion to skillet. Cook, over low heat, until lightly browned. Drain any excess fat. Remove skillet from heat. Crumble bacon into cooked onion. Set aside. Punch dough down. On floured surface, roll into a 15 × 9-inch (37 × 23-cm) rectangle. Spread bacon-onion mixture to within 1 inch (2½ cm) of edges. Roll as you would a jelly roll.

Seal ends. Cut into 1-inch (2½-cm) slices. Place in buttered 12-inch (30-cm) skillet. Cover with warm, damp cloth. Let rise 20 minutes (rolls should not rise too much). Bake at 400° F (200 C) for about 30 minutes, or until golden brown and done. Makes about 14 rolls.

Quick Oatmeal Bread

This recipe produces a biscuitlike bread.

Ingredients:

1 cup (115 g) quick-cooking oats

1¼ (150 g) cups all-purpose flour

2 teaspoons baking powder

¼ teaspoon baking soda

½ teaspoon salt

½ cup (⅛ l) buttermilk

⅓ cup (8 cl) butter, melted

How to prepare:

Spread oats evenly on an ungreased baking sheet. Place under broiler for 3 to 5 minutes, or until lightly browned. Watch carefully so they don't burn. Remove oats from oven and place in mixing bowl. Add flour, baking powder, baking soda, and salt. Stir well. Add buttermilk and butter and stir until a soft dough forms. With hands, shape dough into a ball and place on greased baking sheet. Flatten dough into a 10-inch (25-cm) circle, about ½ inch (1½ cm) thick. Cut circle into 12 small wedges. Bake at 400° F (200 C) in upper third of oven for 12 to 15 minutes. Dip wedges of warm bread into Cheese Fondue or Fondue Bourguignonne. Makes 6 servings.

Fondue Snacks

Ingredients:

1 cup (¼ l) milk

3 tablespoons (45 g) butter

3½ cups (450 g) all-purpose flour

128

1 package (¼ ounce) active dry yeast

1½ teaspoons sugar

½ teaspoon salt

How to prepare:

In small saucepan combine milk and butter. Heat until butter melts. Let cool to lukewarm. In bowl stir together 2½ cups (300 g) flour, yeast, sugar, and salt. Add milk mixture. Beat until well combined. Add enough of remaining flour to form a dough that can be kneaded. Turn out onto a floured board and knead until smooth and elastic. This will take about 8 minutes. Place dough in clean, well-greased bowl. Turn to ensure dough is coated with shortening. Cover with warm, damp cloth. Let rise in warm place until doubled, about 45 minutes. Punch dough down. Shape into a 9-inch (23-cm) loaf. Place in greased 9 × 5 × 3-inch (23 × 15 × 7-cm) loaf pan. Cover with warm, damp towel. Let rise in warm place until doubled, about 30 minutes. Remove towel. Bake at 350° F (180 C) for about 40 minutes, or until well browned and loaf sounds hollow when tapped. Remove from oven and turn loaf out of pan. Let cool 10 to 15 minutes. Break, don't cut, bread into 2-inch (5-cm) pieces. Place on lightly greased baking sheet. Bake at 350° F (180 C) for about 8 minutes, or until light brown. Makes 8 servings.

Baquette or French Bread

Ingredients:

3½ cups (450 g) all-purpose flour

1 tablespoon soy flour

1 package (¼ ounce) active dry yeast

1 teaspoon sugar

1 teaspoon salt

1 cup (¼ l) lukewarm milk

½ cup (⅛ l) lukewarm water

How to prepare:

Combine 2 cups (250 g) all-purpose flour, soy flour, yeast, sugar, and salt in large bowl. Mix well. Add milk and water. Beat until well combined. Add enough of remaining all-purpose flour to form a dough that can be kneaded. Turn out onto a floured board and knead until smooth and elastic. This will take about 8 minutes. Place dough in clean, well-greased bowl. Turn to ensure dough is coated with shortening. Cover with warm, damp cloth. Let rise in warm place until doubled, about 45 minutes. Punch dough down. Divide in half. Shape each half into a 16-inch (40-cm) rope. Place on greased baking sheet. Let rise in warm place until doubled, about 25 minutes. Slash each loaf shallowly and on the diagonal, about 5 or 6 times. Brush with water. Bake at 400° F (200 C) for 25 minutes, or until well browned and done. Makes 2 loaves.

Quick Herb Bread

Ingredients:

1 package (13¾ ounces, 425 g) hot roll mix

1 teaspoon anise or fennel seed, ground with a mortar and pestle

1 cup (¼ l) lukewarm water

How to prepare:

In large bowl combine all ingredients. Stir until dough forms. Turn out onto a floured board. Knead, using additional all-purpose flour, if necessary, until smooth and elastic. This will take about 8 minutes. Place dough in clean, well-greased bowl. Turn to ensure dough is coated with shortening. Cover with a warm, damp cloth. Let rise in warm place until doubled, about 45 minutes. Punch dough down. Shape into a 14-inch (35-cm) long rope. Place on a greased baking sheet. Cover with warm, damp towel and let rise until doubled, about 45 minutes. Slash the top of the loaf with shallow, diagonal cuts (use a very sharp knife or razor blade). Brush with water. Bake at 400° F (200 C) in the middle of the oven, for 40 to 50 minutes, or until golden brown and done. Serve with well-seasoned, not too mild Cheese Fondues, Boiled Meat Fondues, and Variety Meat Fondues. Makes 1 loaf.

Blini Weisham

Ingredients:

1 cup (¼ l) milk

1 tablespoon (15 g) butter

1 package (¼ ounce) active dry yeast

1 teaspoon sugar

1 egg yolk

1 cup (125 g) wholewheat flour

½ teaspoon salt

2 egg whites

How to prepare:

130

In small saucepan combine milk and butter. Heat until butter melts. Let cool to lukewarm. In bowl stir together yeast, sugar, milk mixture, and egg yolk. Add flour and salt. Beat by hand until well combined and fluffy. Cover bowl loosely. Let stand in warm place for about 2 hours, or until doubled in bulk. Stir batter down. It should have the consistency of pancake batter. If too thick, add a tablespoon or 2 of lukewarm water. Beat egg whites until stiff, but not dry. Fold into blini batter. Heat skillet, griddle, or crêpe pan to high temperature (as if you were cooking pancakes). When drops of water added to pan skitter across surface and quickly evaporate, heat is correct. Use a little more than 1 tablespoon of batter to make each blini. When bubbles appear, turn and brown other side. Use while still warm. To dip in fondue, fold blini in half and spear with fork. Excellent with Roquefort Fondue. Makes about 20.

Best Wines and Beers

We have already noted that the more acid the wine for a cheese fondue is, the better. If we stand on the principle that it is always good to drink the same wine with the fondue that was used in the recipe, then dry, tart wines are most suitable.

Since the fondue originated in Switzerland, we believe that the best wines for a cheese fondue are Swiss. Many white wines from Switzerland have a lively, fresh fruitiness combined with very limited sweetness. It can be difficult to find these wines outside of Switzerland—the Swiss like to drink them themselves—but here are a few recommendations: the light white Fendants (a grape variety) from Monthey and Evouette; heavier Fendants and Johannisberg Rieslings from Sierre, Sion, Fully, and Martigny. All Neuchâtel, Lake Geneva, Lake Biel (Bieler See) and Lake Thun (Thuner See) wines. From Neuchâtel and Lake Biel come the so-called "star" wines, whose natural carbonic acid causes the wine to form a delicate star-like design when poured on a surface. These brisk sparkling wines should be served chilled; the cooling is important, since the carbonic acid quickly dissipates if the wine is at room temperature.

Other Swiss whites—the Fendants, the earthy Yvornes and the robust Aigle—should be served slightly warmer with fondue. In any case, it is not necessary to drink an expensive wine, since the cheese flavor is so dominant that the finer points of a great wine are, lost. For this reason we often buy reasonably priced French country wines. Good buys can be found in white Bergerac (from the Dordogne), Edelzwicker (from Alsace), Muscadet de Sevre-et-Maine (from the Loire) or Burgundy's white Mâcon. Also excellent are such German wines as a hearty, tangy Traminer or Silvaner from Frank-

en or Baden. A semi-dry Gutedel or Scheurebe harmonizes nicely with fondue made of well-ripened hard cheese.

We advise white wines for broth fondues with fish or chicken. Here, along with the wines already named, should be mentioned the better grades of white Burgundy or German Auslese if the sauces served are delicate; if the sauces are spicy, beer is more appropriate. With meat fondues, whether cooked in oil or in broth, one can serve an elegant rosé—French or Spanish, German (Weissherbst or Schillerwein), Austrian (Schilcher), or Swiss (Oeil de Perdrix). Here it is a personal choice whether the rosé is dry or sweet.

If you prefer red wines with meat fondues, choose those that are young and fruity. Our favorite is Beaujolais Villages from the négociant Georges Duboeuf, always the previous year's vintage. We drink it at room temperature. Also good is a Bardolino from Verona, a young Rioja from Spain, or a Côtes du Rhône. When the sauces are mild, try a dry red Württemberg Trollinger or an Ingelheim Spätburgunder from Germany. With spicy, heavily seasoned meat and fish fondues, serve beer.

There is an old superstition that beer drunk with cheese fondue will cause stomach problems. Don't believe it. We have enjoyed fondue with everything from Pilsner to Guinness Extra Stout. Beer is also good as the "halfway drink." It is often the best answer with non-cheese fondues as well. Curry sauce, ketchup, and cornichons go better with a light Pilsner than they do with wine.

Remember that all fondues are good with apple wine or hard cider; it is so tart that it can hold its own against strong sauces. Only the driest cider should be served.

An Overview of Fondue Equipment

Fondue fans with room and money can buy a great array of burners, pots, plates, and accessories. Every taste can be satisfied: from rustic to elegant, from ornate to practical.

Begin with a Burner

This is the hero, without which one cannot eat fondue. The smallest burner is a candle: a butter-warmer, food warmer, or tea warmer. The heat from one candle is enough for chocolate fondues, for which a special ceramic set is sold. It should be purchased only if you eat many chocolate fondues, since one can easily improvise with a candlewarmer and heatproof bowls. A food warmer with two candles is appropriate as a warming tray for fondues that do not need more cooking at the table.

Accurate heat is obtained with an alcohol burner. In these burners without wicks the alcohol is poured onto non-flammable glass wool; the flame passes through a sieve and is regulated by means of an air opening. These burners are made of different materials such as tin, copper, and stainless steel. They produce enough heat for cheese or meat fondues, where the cheese mixture or the oil or other cooking liquid is thoroughly heated on the range.

The burner is best bought with its stand to make a complete set. Here the choice is large: the stand may be simple steel or aluminum, practical stainless steel, copper, tempered iron, or heavy rustic cast iron. Do not buy a thin, lightweight stand.

The best burners, on which cooking is clean, odorless, and over controlled heat, are butane-fired. One butane filling will last at high heat for a good hour, at medium heat for three, and at low heat for nine hours. On high heat oil and broth are brought to the boiling point; medium heat keeps them boiling or maintains a braising temperature as for sukiyaki, and low heat keeps food warm. For reasons of safety, gas burners are not sold as a complete set.

A Pot for the Cheese Fondue

The specialized equipment begins here. A pot of glazed clay or ceramic is fine for cheese fondue, though purists insist that it must be unglazed outside and glazed inside like the fondue pots used in the Swiss Jura before the dish became stylish. Though the price of these pots is high, a cheaper pot is not really worth buying; if it is not heat resistant, the fondue will have to be cooked in a saucepan and then poured into the fondue pot for the table. This can make the cheese gummy.

Hairline cracks may appear in a pot glazed on both sides. They need not cause concern if you are careful not to let the pot stand a long time filled with water; if you do, the pores of the clay will soak up the water and may crack when next heated.

A Note on Ceramics

Years ago, information came to us from the U.S. that the glazes of some ceramic dishes are poisonous. In Germany, the U.S.A., and a number of other countries, factory-made ceramic dishes are guaranteed to be free of harmful lead. But we must caution against ceramic pots, bowls, and plates that are brought as souvenirs from southern lands. Since the laws are not as stringent in Mexico, Central and South America, and some Mediterranean countries, the addition of lead to the glazes is a possibility. For the fearful, there are pots for cheese fondue made of enameled aluminum or cast iron.

Less Expensive Equipment

If you want to see first whether you are going to eat a lot of cheese or meat fondues, use any everyday kitchen saucepan. It should be a pot that looks nice and fits well on a burner.

Before you invest in a special pot for oil fondues, use enameled cast iron or steel. You can also prepare a cheese fondue in an enameled pot. Because it conducts heat well, cook the cheese mixture over low heat.

Pots for All Fondues

The classic pots, colored outside and white enamel inside, with thick handles of cast iron or wood, can be used for all kinds of fondues. There are traditional Swiss shapes and modern designs. Specialized meat fondue pots made of copper or stainless steel are available. The copper pots are lined on the inside with tin, stainless steel, or chrome. They transfer heat evenly, are easy to clean, and do not corrode. Such pots will last a whole fondue lifetime. Be sure to have a lid for the fondue pot; you can cover the pot if the oil splashes, and reheat the fondue liquid much more quickly if it cools after a lot of dipping. The lid can also function as a fork holder, with forks hung so that they do not touch the bottom of the pot (this prevents the meat from sticking in an oil fondue). The group can carry on a pleasant conversation while the meat fries by itself. There are also collars with steel fork holders that fit on the abovementioned fondue equipment. Some forks have small hooks on the handle with which they can be hung on the edge of the pot.

Be sure, when buying a pot specially for oil fondues, that the rim is smaller than the bottom to prevent oil splashes from burning your guests. (Bouillon and cheese fondues do not spatter.)

Electric Fondue— Clean and Reliable

For those who do not care overly about the romance of an open flame, the electric fondue is just right. With a thermostatic control, you can prepare chocolate fondue at 140° F, cheese fondue at 170° F, broth fondue at 200° F, and oil or fat fondue at 350° F.

When buying the electric pot, make sure the vessel and the heating element separate for easy cleaning. When turned to its lowest setting, the heating element should be adaptable for use as a warming plate.

Another tip: The machine should have a cord holder so that it cannot be pulled carelessly from the table.

What Else?

The forks for a cheese fondue have long tines and three points. The handles are marked with a dot of color to help diners identify them and to keep from mixing up forks left standing in the pot. The cheese fondue eater only needs one fork; for meat fondue each diner needs two, because forks dipped in hot oil can burn your mouth. Cheese fondue forks can be used for a meat fondue, but special meat fondue forks have only two points, which are barbed so that the meat is not lost in the pot.

Meat skewers made of wood cannot burn the mouth, though they quickly become unsightly. Whatever is used for cooking, the second plate fork can naturally be a regular dinner fork. Perfectionists and ardent fondue fans have special plates—for cheese fondue in the color of the pot or with rustic sayings, and for meat fondue with compartments for the different sauces and salads. A party dish with built-in sauce bowls is also good for meat fondues. Wooden plates are popular as well, although they will become stained by sauces such as curry and mustard.

For those who do not have special plates, fondue can of course still be served on whatever is available. Wooden boards for meat, bread, and such are attractive and inexpensive, and add an appropriate rustic touch to the table.

Important—except for cheese fondue—are small bowls for sauces. They are made by many of the firms manufacturing fondue equipment, in the same colors or of the same material as the rest of the set. You can also use any glass or porcelain bowls of the same size. For those who want it even more coordinated, there is a fondue carousel; the pot sits on a wooden plate in the middle, and around it rotates a second wooden board with glass bowls.

Whether or not to use bibs will depend on the mood of the occasion, but they are a good idea to protect guests from spattering oil fondues.

Watch for the following points before purchasing a pepper mill: Check to see if the grind can be

133

changed from fine to coarse; this is important. Check to see if it can be filled easily. There are mills with such a small filling hole that the peppercorns must be put in one by one—a terrible test of patience. See if the mill turns easily. Most are the type that rotate in themselves, which are easier to manipulate than those that grind with a handle. The mill must not be so small that it disappears in a man's hand, nor so large that it threatens to knock over the fondue pot.

Mills of plastic are not practical, for they get cloudy with time. Mills made of glass are not always easy to find, and sometimes the grinder in them is poor, but at least one can see how much is in them.

As you see, there are lots of choices.

Some Fondue Suggestions

Here are some good fondue ideas
for a range of settings and parties.

For Good Friends:

Glarner Fondue *16*
Gouda Cheese Pot *22*
Bols Fondue *23*
Hermitage Fondue *26*
Lamb Fondue, Syrian
  Style *44*
Asian Fondue *45*
Venison Fondue *46*
California Shrimp
  Fondue *50*
Tempura *52*

Gourmet Fondue *56*
Berlin Lamb Liver
  Fondue *59*
Fish Fondue Theodor
  62
Firepot Weishamer *67*
Sukiyaki, My Style *77*
Bagna Cauda I *88*
Pan Fondue *92*
Whiskey Chocolate
  Fondue *98*

For a Party in the Garden:

Gomser Fondue *16*
Country Fondue *19*
Mainzer Cheese
  Fondue *22*
Beer Fondue *24*
Dill Fondue with
  Seafood *31*
Onion Fondue *30*
Spanish Fondue *33*
Fondue Bourguignonne
  40

Caribbean Meatballs *42*
Bolivian Cheese *43*
German Fish Fondue
  54
Fish Fondue Ulrich
  Klever *63*
Boiled Meat Fondue *71*
Vietnamese Vinegar Pot
  80
Okaribayaki *89*
Lamchi and Boonchi *92*

For a Large Group:

Neuchâtel Fondue *11*
Geneva Fondue I *14*
Ticino Fonduta *19*
Pink Fondue *23*
Raclette *39*
Frikadellen Fondue *42*
Korean Chicken *44*

Mongolian Firepot I *68*
Ten in One Pot *70*
Russian Fondue *72*
Sweet and Sour Pork
  Fondue *83*
Curried Fruit Fondue
  101

For People Who Love the Good Life:

Champagne Fondue *24*
Albese Fonduta with
  Truffles *24*
Hotel Danieli Fonduta
  25
Fondue à la Périgueux
  25
Grand Gala Fondue à
  la Périgueux *26*
Venison Rack Fondue
  46
Strausak Seafood

Fondue *51*
Seafood Fondue Chalet
  Suisse *62*
Oriental Mixed Meat
  Fondue *68*
Chrysanthemum
  Firepot *69*
Vietnamese Firepot *79*
Bagna Cauda II *88*
Asparagus Fondue *90*
Royal Mocha Fondue
  100

For Small and Large Children:

Freiberger Fondue *13*
Pussyfoot Fondue *13*
Buttermilk Fondue *23*
Banana Fondue *33*
Caulifloweret Fondue
  55
Hard-to-Please Fondues
  73

Toblerone Fondue *97*
Mint Chocolate Fondue
  99
Marshmallow Fondue
  100
Butter Nut Fondue *100*
Sweet Tooth Fruit
  Fondue *101*

For Cooks in a Hurry:

Ticino Fondue *19*
Boy Scout or Camping
  Fondue *21*
Sliced Cheese Fondue
  21
Mexican Fondue *34*
Sausage Fondue *35*

Fish Kabob Fondue *50*
Fondue Ranchero *87*
Klever's Tunkis *89*
Sate Ajam Chicken
  Skewers *93*
Simple Ice Cream
  Fondue *103*

Metric—Imperial Conversion Table

Note that the recipes in this book feature both U.S. customary and metric measurements. For cooks in Great Britain, Canada, and Australia, note the following information for imperial measurements. If you are familiar with metric measurements, then we recommend you follow those, incorporated into every recipe. If not, then use these conversions to achieve best results. Bear in mind that ingredients such as flour vary greatly and you will have to make some adjustments.

Liquid Measures

The British cup is larger than the American. The Australian cup is smaller than the British but a little larger than the American. Use the following cup measurements for liquids, making the adjustments as indicated.

U.S.	1 cup (236 ml)
British and Canadian	1 cup (284 ml)—adjust measurement to ¼ pint + 2 tablespoons
Australian	1 cup (250 ml)—adjust measurement to ¼ pint

Weight and Volume Measures

U.S. cooking procedures usually measure certain items by volume, although in other countries these items are often measured by weight. Here are some approximate equivalents for basic items.

	U.S. Customary	Metric	Imperial
Butter	1 cup	250 g	8 ounces
	½ cup	125 g	4 ounces
	¼ cup	62 g	2 ounces
	1 tablespoon	15 g	½ ounce
Flour (sifted all-purpose or plain)	1 cup	128 g	4¼ ounces
	½ cup	60 g	2⅛ ounces
	¼ cup	32 g	1 ounce
Sugar (caster)	1 cup	240 g	8 ounces
	½ cup	120 g	4 ounces
	1 tablespoon	15 g	½ ounce
Chopped vegetables	1 cup	115 g	4 ounces
	½ cup	60 g	2 ounces
Chopped meats or fish	1 cup	225 g	8 ounces
	½ cup	110 g	4 ounces

Index

137